My Hair, My Glory

Is there really any significance?

Juli Jasinski

Cover picture taken by Clay's Photography, Orrville, OH
Models (left to right): Maleah Roudeski, Lorrel Evans, Candice Brewer, Shannon Evans (model on original cover design)

All Scripture quotations are from the Authorized King James Version of the Bible unless otherwise identified.

ISBN 0-9650467-0-2

For information about *My Hair, My Glory*, contact:
Juli Jasinski
31 North Pepperell Road
Hollis, NH 03049
email: Pwrxtrem2@aol.com
Make all checks payable to: Juli Jasinski

First printing, 1995
Second printing, 1996
Third printing, 1997
Fourth printing, 1998
Fifth printing, 2001
Sixth printing, 2013

Printed by:
Pentecostal Publishing House
8855 Dunn Road
Hazelwood, MO 63042

Table of Contents

Acknowledgments

The completion of a project like this could never be the work of the author only. I'm truly grateful to many for your time, help, and encouragement:

• To the Lord first, I thank you with every heartbeat and breath I take. You are everything to me, and I give my life to you.

• To my wonderful husband and covering, without you to shelter, support, and encourage me, my endeavors would be fruitless. I adore you, honey.

• To my pastor, you've been a godly example for me.

• To my dear friends Jeanne Austin and Sharon Nuss, for editing and watching out for all my "p's and q's."

• To Elaine, for your input and encouragement.

• To Joseph King and Todd Williams, for relentlessly helping me in the library and for pointing out where I could find some of the research materials.

• To Gene Guido, my artist and friend, who brings color to my life. You did a fantastic job on the Mary sketch on page 61.

• To two of my most wonderful friends, Donna Pereira and Mae Valentino Pickett, who were there during the struggles of this huge project. Many times you were my shot of adrenalin to the asthmatic trials of my life.

• To Officer Bill Santos, for answering my questions and letting me borrow some papers on criminal information.

• To Ken S. and Carol, my writer friends from OA, for encouraging me to pick up the pen and get writing. Thanks, I needed the push.

• To Sharon Grider, for opening your heart to share some of your experiences.

• To Randolph Nethers and Wholesome Technologies, for your great help in the construction of this book.

• To Scott Fields and Offset Expression, for first printing this book. If it weren't for your wife, Mary Kay, who hungered desperately for the truth of the matter and pushed me to get the book written, the facts would still be lying dormant somewhere on the shelves. Now, hundreds are being fed the truth.

• To Brother Daniel Segraves, a great writer whose voice alone rings of a life full of the love and compassion of Jesus Christ. I appreciate your keeping me within context.

To all of you, I say a heartfelt thank you.

Dedication

This book is affectionately dedicated to all my "sisters in the Lord," and especially to those who have always believed and obeyed the Scripture in I Corinthians 11:6, 14-15, upheld it with confidence, and were not afraid to teach others its principles.

Secondly, I dedicate this book to all those ladies who are in the valley of decision . . . whether or not to cut or to trim. The facts are here. This is truth that will ***make you free*** (John 8:32). Before you grab the shears, read this, and pass the truth on to a friend.

Finally, this book is dedicated to all those who are willing to read this book but did succumb to the temptation to cut your hair, for whatever reason; the Lord knows your heart. He knows you are willing to look at the subject once again.

I humbly choose to ***bear the infirmities of the weak*** (Romans 15:1), and I will continue to be ***always in every prayer of mine for you all making request with joy*** (Philippians 1:4). May you find complete pleasure in serving Him, my friends, ***the eyes of your understanding being enlightened; that ye may know what is the hope of his calling*** (Ephesians 1:18).

Preface

This preface was written to those friends who really do not understand what the hair subject is all about. The apostle Paul wrote many of the books in the New Testament. They were actually letters, better known as "epistles." These epistles were divinely inspired by God to instruct the Christians in the ways of the Lord.

When inspiration comes from the Lord, it's not something spooky to be feared, but it moves on you to take some kind of action. For instance, you or I could be inspired to write a letter to a friend who may be hurting, perhaps from the death of a spouse. Or maybe you'd feel inspired to give someone a call on the phone, only to find out that she was going through one of the most traumatic times in her life. Paul was inspired to write these letters to church members to promote purer Christian living.

All the New Testament letters were written to the already established churches to help them walk closer to God. Second Timothy 3:16 says, ***All scripture is given by inspiration of God, and is profitable for doctrine, for reproof, for correction, for instruction in righteousness.*** We can read this verse better this way: "All scripture is *theopneustos*," which means, in Greek, it is "God-breathed." God breathed on each author to write, or, better, He inspired them to write the words of Scripture in each book of the Bible.

Therefore, the words of all Scripture are to be received as they are from God Himself. This method of communication of God's Word to man is evidence that the desire of God was to reach man with His truth so we may find our way to heaven.

The fact that it was "breathed out" by God makes it clearer that it is 'profitable' to us in four ways: 1) "for doctrine"—to know what to believe, 2) "for reproof"—to discern what not to believe, 3) "for correction"—to learn what not to do, 4) "for instruction in righteousness"—to understand what should be done (Criswell, study notes, 1355).

In the first book of Corinthians, Paul was writing to the members of the church in the city of Corinth. In this epistle, he focused on the various problems their church was having and delivered to its members some solutions to the dilemmas.

The eleventh chapter of the first book of Corinthians deals with three areas: (1) the divine order for marriage, (2) propriety in worship, (3) the Lord's Supper. He also included some verses on the appearances of hair and how it was to be groomed by Christian men and women. The command was simple: men, keep your hair cut short; and, ladies, keep your hair uncut and long (I Corinthians 11:13-15).

Many of today's Christians don't acknowledge or even realize that there is any significance to this passage. Many times these few verses are overlooked for one reason or another. The esoteric interest in hair should not be confined to only a few Spirit-filled believers, but it should be known to all who wish to serve the Lord Jesus and walk in His ways. However, there is actually a tug-of-war going on in Christendom over hair length. I won't debate the meaning of the verses but expound on the discoveries to the significances of the lady's hair. This book teaches, along with the revealing significances of hair, God's intended purpose for hair. (See chapter eight.)

God's Word speaks candidly of His plan for the church. The Scriptures help us to know truly what to believe. His principles are made clear for all to comprehend. For example, the way of salvation is not complex or complicated but quite plain and simple. It's found in the Book of the Acts of the Apostles. Chapter 2, verse 38, simply states: ***Then Peter said unto them, Repent, and be baptized every one of you in the name of Jesus Christ for the remission of sins, and ye shall receive the gift of the Holy Ghost***.

However, this just allows you to get on the path of the redeemed. The rest is revealed in God's Word to teach you to walk closer to Jesus in the ways of holy living and, eventually, to make it to heaven. After all, isn't that our goal?

Introduction

It has been both a challenge and a blessing to write on the subject of lady's hair. Originally, I was planning to write a simple pamphlet or a booklet, but I kept getting more and more information on this subject. Now, it's become a book. This book came out of a desire to record some very interesting findings that took over two years of research on the subject. My primary purpose is to answer the question: "My hair, my glory, is there really any significance?" It is the hope of the author that the reader, after reading each chapter, will have a definite answer to that very contemplative question.

This book was intended to be written as an expository work. My effort was simply to educate its readers on the significance of lady's hair and whether the facts were influenced or not by the biblical teaching found in I Corinthians 11. My aim was to present the information in four separate categories: spiritual, biblical, historical, and criminal. The information given in these categories support the fact that there is significance to a lady's hair. It is my goal for this book to inform, not to persuade its readers.

This book does not discuss semantics. In his book, *Hair Length in the Bible*, Rev. Daniel Segraves does more than a thorough and comprehensive job on the passage of Scripture in I Corinthians 11:5-15. He takes each portion of Scripture, dissects it piece by piece, and explains it so that one can understand the meaning of each verse. It would be redundant if I were to do that.

Two other popular works are *In Search of Holiness* and *Practical Holiness: A Second Look*, written by Revs. Loretta Bernard and David Bernard. These two books give the strong scriptural meanings and their symbolic implications of hair in the Bible. They will leave you with no doubts. I have no desire to repeat their work.

Writing this book has truly been rewarding for me in many ways. It is my prayer that the information provided will help clear any confusion over to whether or not there is significance to the woman's hair. All who read this book, both men and women, will be able to strengthen their conviction and firmly conclude that there is a greater deal of significance to the lady's hair than one has realized before.

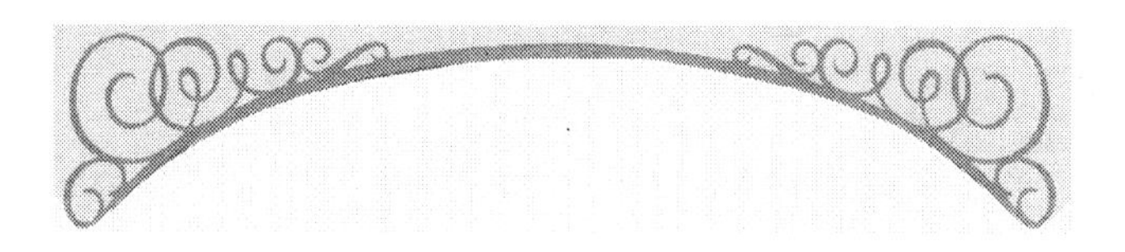

1 – The Search Begins

The Hungarian-born writer, Arthur Koestler, once wrote, "The more original a discovery, the more obvious it seems afterwards." Although the discovery of the significance of the woman's hair is not original, it will, however, seem very obvious. Yet it's not that obvious to some because they are having a real battle over it to the point, unfortunately, that some churches have even split.

The Lord showed me the women's hair principle in I Corinthians 11:2-16 shortly after my conversion. I learned that He wanted me to keep my hair long and uncut as a sign of submission to His authority. I've never really been tempted to challenge His Word, so I just let my shoulder-length hair grow out. Some of my friends, however, wrestled daily with submission to His Word.

The tension I felt between us was getting worse. A spirit of confusion was beginning to grow. Many were asking me what I thought the Scriptures meant about this subject, hoping to find answers. I prayed earnestly that the Lord would help me understand what was going on and why there was so much doubt in the minds of my friends.

Then the whole thing exploded like fireworks.

All the discoveries I found caused this book to be born. This is how it all started.

I never really gave the hair question much thought; I just believed that God's Word says what it says! *It's simple*, I thought. *Believe, pray, and obey.* Then one noteworthy day, May 19, 1993, when I was at a friend's funeral, my curiosity got stirred up. I saw many of my old worldly friends, and as usual, they were all drinking beer and smoking pot. Nothing had changed with them. Seeing them reminded me of how it used to be. They were full of the things of this world, empty and lost.

We all shared the same grief and dismay at the loss of our old friend, Dolly. I knew her for almost thirty years. She and I spent eight years together at the same Catholic school. We had sat in the same classrooms and had the same teachers from the first grade all the way through the eighth grade.

It couldn't be! Who would have thought that Dolly was the next to die in our group of friends? It was a miserable fact. She just married a nice fellow three years before, and just two years ago she had her first baby girl. It was so sad to think that her daughter would never know her mommy. Our hearts ached with pain. We wiped away the tears, giving each other the appropriate hugs.

Dolly's family picture

After the funeral, the old gang and I decided to go down the street to a country deli, where we sat for hours talking and laughing about the good ol' days we had during high school. The memories were plentiful, and nobody tried to dig up the old dirt of the past that wasn't worth discussing. We still had fun reminiscing.

One woman there, however, made it her business to make fun of me in front of everybody every time she had a chance. She remembered what I was like and, perhaps, could not stand the change the Lord had made in my life.

She was an old friend who never got over some things of the past for which she was responsible. She and one other woman who was present were involved with the New Age movement and its beliefs. I overheard them talking about herbs, crystals, auras, and so on. So later I figured the tension I felt must have been because their spirits didn't like the Holy Spirit within me.

It was finally time to go home. We had a two-hour drive to our hometown. I made the rounds to say good-bye to everyone. The friend I drove with to the funeral was in the parking lot with these two women, smoking another joint for the road.

As I walked closer, I prayed under my breath, pleading the blood of Jesus for their souls. They, however, made snide remarks because I didn't want to join to smoke the joint. They made gestures as if I were a "goody two-shoes" or a perfect little angel.

Bless their hearts; they didn't know what they were doing. I just smiled and thought, *No way, praise God! I don't want that dead-end life again.* I knew what the Lord had done for me in my life. I found something certainly a billion times greater than drinking beer and doing drugs. This new life I found in Jesus Christ has kept me more than sixteen years. Who would want to go back to that miserable life again? To God be the glory for the things He has done for me!

The woman who made all the cutting remarks in the deli made an interesting comment to me that caused a Holy Ghost explosion in my soul. Her remark was actually the basis for me to spend more than two years of study and research on the subject of hair. The encounter went something like this:

I had worn my hair down that day. She walked up to me, stroked my hair, and said, "Oooh, Juli, your hair is longer than mine; don't you know that your hair holds energy?"

"Oh, really?" I replied. "That's nice."

I didn't ask any further questions about what she understood about hair, but I wondered if the New Agers like herself were aware of the power that is promised in the Bible to women who submit themselves to God by not cutting their hair. I thought, *You mean, we Oneness Pentecostals are not the only ones out there who believe that there is power on a woman's head "because of the angels"?*

Questions began to flood my mind as my eyes gazed out the car window. What do the New Agers know? Do they understand the source of the power? When did they find out? Do the occult and other religions believe in the hair principle? Do they believe that there is significance to a lady's hair?

On the way home, I began thinking that there must be more to I Corinthians 11:15 than we really understand. "I have to find out," I determined. I was still pondering if there could be any significance to this hair thing or if it is just a verse on pure obedience. If the New Agers won't cut their hair because of "energy," is there a power principle they follow, too?

There must be something to that Bible verse. I wondered if there really was, so I decided to start researching it at once. My discoveries mounted higher and higher until finally the research piled into an irrefutable mountain of evidence. Wow, I couldn't believe my eyes at all the spiritual findings! As you read the following examples, you will find amazing pagan significances to women's hair in the world of the occult.

Spiritual Findings in Pagan Significance

The pagan significance of hair was the most difficult part of my study. As I ripped off the cover, diving into the New Age movement, I had much to wade through in the cesspool of occult sciences, witchcraft, and other types of spiritualism in order to find any information. Fortunately, many friends prayed for me as I began my search. Each day before I started to dive into the research, I prayed over my mind, covering it with the blood of Jesus. I asked the Lord to surround me with His angels.

I decided to go directly to the public library to look in the witchcraft section. As I approached the occult section, I could feel the demonic spirits. First, I prayed against the wickedness I sensed and anointed with oil the area containing the occult books so that I could think clearly to start my search. To my surprise, I found many, many references concerning hair. I was amazed and, at times, dumbfounded! I thought, *If only Christians knew what the witches know!* Later, I told a friend that if today's Christians knew this, they might view this subject in a different light. At one point, I asked a good friend of mine to come with me to a metaphysical bookstore in Santa Cruz, the heart of central California's witch haven. She got a firsthand look at all the information herself. She, too, marveled at the voluminous sight.

According to the *Encyclopedia of Superstition, Folklore and the Occult Sciences of the World*, "women's hair is a most precious amulet and wards off a great many evils and diseases."[1] Derek and Julia Parker say in their book, *The Power of Magic Secrets and Mysteries Ancient*

---

1. Cora Linn Daniels and Prof. C. M. Stevans, PhD (eds.), *Encyclopedia of Superstition, Folklore and the Occult Sciences of the World*, vol. 1 (1903; Detroit: Gale Research Company, 1971), 282.

and Modern, "Hair has always been considered strong magic; witches casting an evil spell needed a piece of hair from their victim to make it truly efficacious."[2]

Barbara Walker writes in one of her books, *The Women's Dictionary of Symbols and Sacred Objects*, "Women's hair carried heavy symbolic and spiritual significance in Oriental Religions. Tantric sages proclaimed that the binding or unbinding of women's hair could control cosmic powers of creation and destruction."[3]

In another book, Walker states, "As shown by its importance in witch-charms and in the mutual exchange of talismans between lovers, hair was usually viewed a repository of at least a part of the soul."[4]

In discussing the significance of hair, Harry E. Wedeck and Wade Baskin state in their book, *Dictionary of Spiritualism*, "In occultism and mystic philosophy, the hair, both human and animal is regarded as the receptacle of the vital essence."[5] In their other book, *Dictionary of Pagan Religions*, Wedeck and Baskin write "with various sects, cutting of the hair and beard has been regarded as a sign of defilement."[6]

Many Hindus believe that the hair on their head is sacred and therefore will not cut it. "A number of sects left the hair completely unshorn like a woman's," says Benjamin Walker in his book, *The Hindu World: An Encyclopedic Survey of Hinduism*, "in the belief that when the hair reached a certain length the vital forces of the body were no longer diverted to assist in its further growth, and the surplus energy

---

2. Derek Parker and Julia Parker, *The Power of Magic Secrets and Mysteries Ancient and Modern* (New York: Simon and Schuster, 1992), 74.

3. Barbara Walker, "Hair," *The Women's Dictionary of Symbols and Sacred Objects* (San Francisco: Harper & Row, 1988), 313.

4. Barbara Walker, "Hair," *The Woman's Encyclopedia of Myths and Secrets* (1983), 367.

5. Harry E. Wedeck and Wade Baskin, "Hair," *Dictionary of Spiritualism* (New York: Philosophical Library, 1971), 167.

6. Harry E. Wedeck and Wade Baskin, "Hair," *Dictionary of Pagan Religions* (New York: Philosophical Library, 1971), 143.

added to one's virility."[7] He continues, "Among contemporary semi-Hindu sects the Sikhs never shave or cut the hair of the body, and some sadhus and yogis observe the same prohibition."[8]

Many orthodox Muslim women also wear their hair long and uncut. However, for the Roman Catholic nun, shaving her head supposedly signifies her humiliation and renunciation of the world. Buddhists priests also have shaved their head as to appear less attractive to others.[9]

A noted doctor of metaphysical and holistic disciplines, June G. Bletzer, writes, "Hair has psychical powers that act as a protection from evil entities of the etheric world; cutting of the hair was done in a ritual to discontinue this protection; it is symbolic of strength."[10] She adds, "It contributes to one's personality, and is a mark of identification; to shave one's head is to remove one's self-image so one can begin a new self-image."[11]

"Hair was assumed to have magical properties of its own," says *Man, Myth, and Magic*, "and was surrounded with its own system of magical rites, devised for the purpose of protecting the head from psychic injury and of protecting those who had the task of dressing or cutting the hair from the anger of the indwelling spirits."[12] Additionally, it states, "Superstition was that human strength resided in the hair and

---

7. Benjamin Walker, "Head," *The Hindu World: An Encyclopedic Survey of Hinduism*, vol. 1 (New York: Frederick A. Praeger Publishers, 1968), 433.

8. Ibid.

9. Wedeck and Baskin, *Dictionary of Pagan Religions*, 144.

10. June G. Bletzer, "Hair," *The Donning International Encyclopedic Psychic Dictionary* (Virginia: Donning Company, 1986), 269.

11. Ibid.

12. Richard Cavendish (ed.), "Hair," *Man, Myth, and Magic*, vol. 5 (Freeport Long Island: Marshall Cavendish Corp., 1983), 1201.

that cutting it reduced bodily vitality."[13]

"Since ancient times, hair and nails have been thought to possess magical attributes that have made them important ingredients in many magic spells," says Rosemary Ellen Guiley, in her book, *Encyclopedia on Witches and Witchcraft*. "Hair has been associated with strength and virility, and with psychic protection."[14] Guiley continues, "A witch's magical power is bound in her hair; by shaking her hair in the wind, the power of a spell is doubled."[15]

According to the *Encyclopedia of Occultism and Parapsychology*, "Hair has had an occult significance since ancient times. . . . It has been regarded as a source of strength. The association of hair with sexual features of the body has given it remarkable force, and distinctions between male and female hair have emphasized sexual attraction. The unisex fashions of the permissive society and rock groups have tended to create sexual confusion and neurotic behavior."[16] The revolt of the '60s will be discussed in chapter seven.

"Since the hair is believed to be intimately related to the life of an individual, it has magical significance in witchcraft rituals, and many civilizations have been at pains to prevent their hair falling into the hands of an enemy, who might use it for black magic ill-wishing. There is a school of character reading from the hair, known as trichsomancy."[17]

In ancient Mexico, girls wildly tossed their unbound hair in ritual dances in honor of the maize goddess, the "long-haired mother," as this encouraged a luxuriant growth of the maize [corn] crop.[18]

According to Wendy Cooper, author of the book, *Hair: Sex, Society, Symbolism*, so "widespread was the faith in the power of hair

---

13. Ibid.

14. Rosemary Ellen Guiley, "Hair & Nails," *Encyclopedia on Witches and Witchcraft* (New York: Facts on File, 1989), 148-149.

15. Ibid.

16. Leslie A. Shepard (ed.), "Hair," *Encyclopedia of Occultism and Parapsychology*, 2nd ed., vol. 3 (Detroit: Gale Research Company, 1984), 572.

17. Ibid.

18. Cavendish, 1201.

. . . that in Scotland it was ominous even to meet a woman with her hair uncovered. . . . If a woman shook her hair at you, they believed anything could happen."[19]

"One of the most common uses of hair," says the *Encyclopedia of Religion*, "is in hostile magical; the hair clippings of an intended victim are obtained, and ensorcelled . . . and mixed together with other bodily secretions."[20]

Infamous black magician, Aleister Crowley secretly hid his hair and nail clippings throughout his life.[21] The belief was "whoever possessed another's hair had power over his soul."[22] In Ozark lore, hair combings are buried, never thrown out. French peasants bury hair; Turks and Chileans stuff hair clippings into walls.[23]

The fifteenth-century German inquisitor Jacob Sprenger was satisfied with merely shaving the heads of witches before they were cast into the flames.[24] In Bastar, a woman or a man suspected of sorcery was beaten by the crowd and the head shaved, supposedly constituting the power of that one's mischief. Later the hair was attached to a tree in some public place for all eyes to see.[25]

Believing that it was the will of heaven, Joan of Arc, who said she heard from Michael the archangel, Saint Catherine, and Saint Margaret, renounced woman's dress to wear the attire of a man. Many people of that day feared her transvestitism. Joan claimed she had "divine guidance" that refuted the prohibition of Deuteronomy 22:5, "declaring that the new dispensation has canceled the old; and her special circumstances require special responses."[26] According to Warner, Joan of Arc believed the voices were from heaven, and that "she was chosen to bear

---

19. Wendy Cooper, *Hair: Sex, Society, Symbolism* (New York: Stein and Day, 1971), 197.
20. Mircea Eliade (ed.), "Hair," *Encyclopedia of Religion*, vol. 6 (New York: MacMillan, 1987), 156.
21. Guiley, 149.
22. Barbara Walker, *Myths and Secrets*, 369.
23. Guiley, 149.
24. Cooper, 197.
25. Ibid.
26. Marina Warner, *Joan of Arc: The Image of Female Heroism* (New York: Alfred A. Knopf, 1981), 146.

His standard; and she cut off her hair in order to accomplish the salvation of the French. Saint Paul's ban in I Corinthians 11:14-15 is overturned in her case."[27] Upon her capture, she refused to wear the attire of a woman and all that was associated with femininity.[28] "It was the clergy who was jealous of her familiarity with angels," declare Henry and Dana Lee Thomas, in *Living Biographies of Famous Women*.[29] Many of her followers in the end turned against her, believing that she was the devil-inspired witch of Domremy.[30]

The Bhils of Central India tortured suspected witches, then cut off their hair and buried it, thus severing the link between the witches and their magical power. In the Middle Ages, witches were shaved in the belief that it rendered them powerless and more likely to confess.[31] Many practices like these have been almost universal among primitive tribes throughout the world with different variations.[32]

The most powerful reason for caution on the part of primitive peoples, when it came to cutting their hair, was their widely held belief in homeopathic and sympathetic magic. Homeopathic magic involved the production of an effect simply by imitating it. In Laos, when an elephant hunter started out, his wife was forbidden to cut her hair, because he believed that the elephant could sever any ropes that were used to restrain him.[33]

"In Leitrim, while some peasants burn their hair and nails for fear of the fairies, others kept their hair-cuttings, which they thought may be required on the Day of Judgment to turn the scale against the weight of sins," says *Encyclopedia of Religion* and *Ethics*.[34] The original fear was that the body should not appear incomplete on the Day of Judgment but

---

27. Ibid.
28. Ibid., 144.
29. Henry Thomas and Dana Lee Thomas, *Living Biographies of Famous Women* (New York: Garden Ciy, 1942), 45.
30. Ibid.
31. Guiley, 149.
32. Cooper, 208, 215.
33. Ibid., 213.
34. James Hastings (ed.), "Hair & Nails," *Encyclopedia of Religion and Ethics*, vol. 6 (New York: Charles Scribner's Sons, 1955), 475.

how God created it.[35]

If you look through a book on ancient religions, you will note that most of the pagan gods and goddesses were long-haired. Many of the pagan worshipers devised their gods with profuse hair. The early Aryan settlers of India worshiped the sun that they addressed as "the golden-haired," and the ancient hymns of the Hindu sacred book, *Rig-Veda*, describes the solar god as "the brilliant sun with flaming hair." The same symbol of luxuriant locks adorned other sun-gods; the Rhidian Helios, the Greek Apollo, the American Tzontemoc, the Gaulish Cunobelin, and many more gods had similar hairy looks.[36] Many pagans believe the hair on the goddess Isis carried magical powers of protection, resurrection, and reincarnation. An Egyptian found salvation by identifying himself with Osiris her son, for whom the goddess made resurrection magic with her hair. She further protected her divine child, Osiris, "by shaking out her hair over him."[37]

The goddess worshipers have a distorted view of what they call signs and wonders. They believe that a comet was supposed to be a tendril of the Great Mother's hair appearing in the sky as the world was slowly overshadowed by the brilliance of the celestial body.

Goddess worshipers also have an idea among prophetic priestesses or witches, who supposedly operated with unbound hair on the theory that their tresses could control the spirit world. They say that the Mother Goddesses—like Isis, Cybele, and many emanations of Kali—commanded the weather by braiding or releasing their hair. The verse, Matthew 16:19, ***whatsoever thou shalt bind on earth shall be bound in heaven: and whatsoever thou shalt loose on earth shall be loosed in heaven***, was greatly distorted in Europe when they believed witches' hair controlled the weather.[38]

"St. Paul," Barbara Walker writes, "greatly feared the 'angels' (spirits) that women could command by letting their hair flow loose, he insisted that women's heads be covered in church lest they draw demons

35. Ibid.
36. Cooper, 185.
37. Barbara Walker, *Myths and Secrets*, 367.
38. Ibid., 368.

into the building." In referring to I Corinthians 11:10, Walker interprets ***because of the angels*** to mean the spirits were supposed to be attracted or controlled by unbound female hair.[39]

These are only forty of the many examples showing that hair holds great significance in the world of spiritualism, occultism, and paganism. I was surprised that almost all these pagan references refer to Bible passages, including the story of Samson and the verses in I Corinthians 11 concerning hair.

This leads me to believe that the devil knows exactly what God intended for the woman and her hair. The devil, however, wanted to use it for his evil purposes, but God wants it to be used for our good. Many of today's Bible commentaries and study Bibles cite further references that in ancient days the women's hair was to be kept long.

What Bible Commentaries, Encyclopedias, Dictionaries, and Study Bibles Say

"The hair's capacity for constant growth," says the *Interpreter's Dictionary of the Bible*, "has always made it seem an important seat of life and, therefore, religiously significant."[40]

The *Illustrated Bible Dictionary* refers to the normal custom of the Israelites, both sexes, to let their hair grow long, but by the time of the New Testament, long hair was "shame" to a man, which Paul stated to the church in Corinth.[41] We'll discuss the Corinthian church in chapter four.

The *Unger's Bible Dictionary* states, "The Hebrews bestowed special care on the hair and beard, regarding thick, abundant hair as an ornament. . . . Women always wore their hair long."[42] The *Collins Gem Dictionary of the Bible* says, "Hebrew women were generally black

---

39. Ibid.

40. "Hair," *Interpreter's Dictionary of the Bible*, supp. vol. (Nashville: Abingdon, 1976), 512.

41. J. D. Douglas, MA, BD, STM, PhD (ed.), "Hair," *Illustrated Bible Dictionary*, vol. 2 (1962; Wheaton: Tyndale House, 1980), 600.

42. Merrill F. Unger, "Hair," *Unger's Bible Dictionary* (Chicago: Moody Press, 1966), 440.

haired, wearing long braided or unbraided tresses often with ornaments."[43] Excessive wearing of ornaments on the body and in the hair was the common ancient fashion. These hairdos usually took at least six to eight hours to fix.

This may be the reason the apostle Peter wrote,

> ***Whose adorning let it not be that outward adorning of plaiting the hair, and of wearing of gold, or of putting on of apparel; but let it be the hidden man of the heart, in that which is not corruptible, even the ornament of a meek and quiet spirit, which is in the sight of God of great price*** (I Peter 3:3, 4).

The *Eerdman's Bible Dictionary* states, "Nevertheless, long hair appears to have been the rule among the Hebrews, both men and women. . . . In New Testament times, Palestine men adopted the Roman style of closely cropped hair, whereas long hair was deemed appropriate for women."[44] The *Westminster Dictionary of the Bible* states plainly, "Hebrew women wore their hair long, binding it up or braiding it."[45]

The *Matthew Henry Commentary* records, "The woman's hair is a natural covering; to wear it long is a glory to her; but for a man to have long hair is a token of

---

43. James L. Dow, MA, "Hair," *Collins Gem Dictionary* (1974; London and Glasgow: Collins, 1987), 208.

44. Allen C. Myers (rev. ed.), "Hair," *Eerdman's Bible Dictionary* (Grand Rapids: William B. Eerdman, 1987), 455.

45. Henry Snyder Gehman (ed.), "Hair," *New Westminster Dictionary of the Bible* (Philadelphia: Westminster Press, 1970), 357.

softness and effeminacy."[46]

The *Zondervan Parallel New Testament in Greek and English Bible* says in the Greek interlinear that the exact transcription of I Corinthians 11:14, 15 is as follows: ***Not nature [her]self teaches you that a man indeed if he wears his hair long, a dishonour to him it is, but a woman if she wears her hair long, a glory to her it is, because the long hair instead of a veil has been given to her.***[47]

The *Criswell Study Bible* says, "The covered head was the symbol of a woman's submission to her own husband; to fail to acknowledge publicly this headship was a disgrace of such magnitude as to be equal to having a shorn head, which was in antiquity the symbol of a shameless, dishonored woman."[48] The *Harper's Bible Commentary* states, "Women prophets and pneumatics are admonished to wear their hair bound up like a crown rather than unbound, since this was in Greco-Roman understanding, a sign of frenzy, and in Jewish understanding, a sign of adultery. Disheveled hair was as disgraceful for a woman as for her head to be shaven."[49]

According to the *Harper's Encyclopedia of Bible Life*, "Nothing definite is known about the hair styling of Jewish women: they do not appear in the monumental and funerary art that has survived as do Egyptian, Greek, and Roman women. Biblical writers deplored the excessive ornamentation of the hair."[50] Even in ancient times, God didn't want His women to be of the world, making themselves a reputation. They were to be as Jesus, who ***made himself of no reputation*** (Philippians 2:7).

The *Jewish Encyclopedia* declares, "Among women long hair is extolled as a mark of beauty. A woman's hair was never cut except as

---

46. Leslie R. Church, PhD, F.R. Hist. S. (ed.), *Matthew Henry Commentary* (1960; Grand Rapids: Zondervan, 1980), 1817.

47. *Zondervan Parallel New Testament in Greek and English* (1975; Grand Rapids: Zondervan, 1980), 507.

48. W. A. Criswell, PhD (ed.), study notes, *Criswell Study Bible* (1975; Nashville: Thomas Nelson, 1979), 1355.

49. James L. Mays (ed.), "Women Prophets," *Harper's Bible Commentary* (San Francisco: Harper & Row, 1988), 1183.

50. Madeleine S. Miller & J. Lane Miller (eds.), "Hairdressing," *Harper's Encyclopedia of Bible Life*, 3rd ed. (San Francisco: Harper & Row, 1978), 86.

a sign of deep mourning or of degradation. . . . Originally, shaving the head in times of mourning indicated that the hair was sacrificed to the dead."[51] Although shaving of the head in deep mourning was an accepted custom in Israel, it was prohibited by the Mosaic law on the grounds that God's people belong to Yahweh only[52] (Deuteronomy 14:1, 2; Leviticus 21:5; Jeremiah 7:29).

The twelve Bible commentaries and study Bibles I researched mention that the woman's hair was kept long, implying that it was neither cut short nor touched with any cutting instruments for cosmetic reasons. However, there was a time when, in order "to dishonor" and "to disgrace" a woman, her head was shaved.

The Disgraced Head

God's desire for His people was that they remain chaste and pure until they married. Fidelity was ordered by God in the seventh commandment.

In his book, *The World of Ancient Israel*, David Meilsheim reports, "When a woman was accused and found guilty of adultery, her hair was cut or her head shaved." He continues by saying, "The following formula was used: 'Because you have scorned the customs of the daughters of Israel, who walk with their's covered, what you have chosen has happened to you.' " Meilsheim accredits this as a "throwback to the ancient faith of the Israelites who believed that evil spirits came to dominate women who went bare-headed."[53]

Disheveling the hair or covering it with dirt, ashes, or mud were all signs of mourning. When a person wanted to convey deeply felt grief, he would completely shave the head or ***make baldness upon their head*** (Leviticus 21:5). The shorn head on both a woman or man was a common practice among many nations, including the Hebrew people

---

51. Isidore Singer, PhD (ed.), "Hair," *The Jewish Encyclopedia*, vol. 6 (New York: KTAV Publishing House, 1965), 158.

52. Ibid.

53. David Meilsheim, Grace Jackman (trans.), *The World of Ancient Israel* (New York: Tudor, 1973), 84.

even though they were forbidden to do this by the Lord God. Job shaved his head as a sign of his mourning the death of his sons and daughters (Job 1:20).

In Ezra, we find an example of the grief experienced by this prophet. Instead of shaving his head, he pulled or yanked his hair out. ***And when I heard this thing, I rent my garment and my mantle, and plucked off the hair of my head and of my beard, and sat down astonied*** (Ezra 9:3).

He could not believe what he heard about the iniquity that had penetrated the nation of Israel. His intense expression of anguish was demonstrated by actions leading him to a deep, agonizing intercession and confession for the people of God.

The Lord instructed the men of Israel that if they took a wife who was captive, she should shave her head in the rite of purification and initiation (to the tribe). In addition, it was required by the law that the leper had to shave his head in the day of his cleansing (Deuteronomy 21:12; Leviticus 14:8-9).

Shaving the head was not only an ancient punishment executed in ancient days but also has been practiced through the centuries to recent years. My father, Jacob Vanden Berge, is a survivor of World War II. When the war ended, there was great rejoicing throughout all the streets of Europe and in his city, Rotterdam. In the midst of the countries' exuberance, mayhem struck the hearts of men. Swift retribution was made for the collaboration of their women with the Nazi soldiers.

My father related his story. One day on Prins Hendrikade, the street he lived on, he and some of his buddies combed the street, going door to door, looking for any of these women who fraternized with the Nazis. He said that during the war they kept a mental note of these women who got involved in this abhorrently permissive conduct. When the war was over, the hometown boys vowed that these women would pay for their actions.

Upon finding such a girl, one boy grabbed a chair, a pair of scissors, and a feather pillow from her house while my father and another boy dragged her outside. They proceeded to disgrace her by shaving her head. And that was not enough. They spread tar on her head and covered it with feathers. These three eighteen-year-old boys did this to four of the girls who lived on their street. Unbeknownst to my father, this was happening throughout other streets of Europe as well.

In a town outside Paris, many of the guilty women were stripped first, then put on a wooden platform in front of the townspeople for all to see. A French GI made a ceremony out of the shaving of one woman's hair. He forced the woman to look at herself in a mirror in front of a large, jeering crowd.

The Scandal of Hitler

Even worse were the appalling atrocities at Auschwitz during World War II. The infamous Adolf Hitler was possessed with legions of devils. His inhumane behavior toward the Jews is so mind-boggling that it's almost hard to believe the accounts are true. Through Hitler, the devil knew how to ridicule God's people and His holy Word.

The first thing Hitler said was that he renounced the idea of conscience and mocked the concept of circumcision. He instructed the German people to burn all Jewish books, including the Bible. The highest insult he could spew out was to call the Jews, pigs; some were made to stand on street corners wearing signs around their necks saying "I'm a pig. I am vermin." In reenacting the wicked Haman, Hitler hung ten Jews in gallows built just as the Book of Esther described.

The most outrageous act was when he had all the women and girls shaved upon their arrival at the concentration camps. The devil knew how to strip the women of their glory and power. At the liberation of

Auschwitz in January 1945, seven tons of hair were found in the camp's warehouses.[54] The hair was intended to manufacture haircloth. Some of the hair came from victims of gassing. Cracow Institute of Judicial Expertise analyzed the hair and found traces of prussic acid, a poisonous component typical of Zyklon compounds, present in the hair. Often even the inmates whose hair had been allowed to grow back during their time in the camps had their corpses scalped before they were placed on the incinerators.[55]

Shaving the Head in Idolatrous Worship

According to John L. McKenzie in his book, *Dictionary of the Bible*, "It is well known that among the Gentile nations that surrounded Israel the hair of childhood or youth was often shaved and consecrated at idolatrous shrines. Frequently this custom marked an initiatory rite into the service of a divinity. To the Jew it was therefore an abomination of the Gentiles."[56]

Both in Arabia and in Syria, the custom was to sacrifice hair as an initiation into the state of adolescence.[57] Many vestal virgins in the Greek culture performed a ritual of shaving their head on reaching puberty to dedicate it to their river god. The significance of hair sacrifice was made explicit in the rites at the temple of Astare, Phoenician goddess of fertility, at Byblos. The great anthropologist Sir James Frazer, in *The Golden Bough*, wrote, "Here, at the annual mourning for the dead Adonis, the women have to shave their heads, and such of them as refused to do so were bound to prostitute themselves to strangers and to sacrifice to the goddess with the wages of their shame."[58]

The cutting of hair in times past was a means whereby the living were put in direct communion with the dead. Often the mourner's hair

---

54. Teresa Swiebocka, Jonathan Weber and Connie Wilsack (trans.), *Auschwitz: A History in Photographs* (Poland: Panstwowe, 1990), 25.
55. Ibid.
56. John L. McKenzie, S.J., "Hair in Idol Worship," *Dictionary of the Bible* (New York: Bruce, 1965), 597.
57. Hastings, 476.
58. Cooper, 66.

was placed on the tomb, in the grave, or on the corpse itself. However, this custom has been forgotten in days gone by; now the mourner only shaves his or her hair as a mere expression of grief. The Persians would cut not only their own hair but also that of their horses after the death of a famous general.[59]

Bald Was Beautiful?

Israel's heathen neighbors, especially Egypt, held contempt for anyone who was hairy and unshaved. These early Egyptians shaved their heads completely on a regular basis for cosmetic reasons. Author James Putnam writes, "Shaving was seen as a way of cleansing the spirit, and ancient Egyptian priests and priestesses all shaved their heads."[60]

This was a time when the ancient world thought bald was beautiful. Wealthy women and men visited barbers regularly. Some owned slaves who would dress their hair daily. It is said that Cleopatra at that time owned 149 wigs. Egyptians abhorred natural long hair so much that they only grew it back during a time of mourning.[61]

The Lord Jehovah did not want the children of Israel to get caught up in any pagan worship but to avoid it altogether. We can see by these examples that shaving the hair on one's head was not only practiced in the ancient cultures but repeated in recent years, and it may still be performed in third-world countries today. It was not only used as a punishment, to disgrace a woman's head, or to demonstrate a time of mourning but was also used in idolatrous worship and for cosmetic reasons.

It's no wonder God instructed the Israelites not to shave their heads but to keep their hair long. ***They shall not make baldness upon their head, neither shall they shave off the corner of their beard, nor make any cuttings in their flesh*** (Leviticus 21:5). He wanted to show the world that His people were a separate, holy nation called out to give glory to His name alone.

---

59. Hastings, 476.

60. James Putnam, *Mummy* (1992; New York: Alfred A. Knopf, 1993), 47.

61. Bill Severn, *The Long and Short of It: 5000 Years of Fun and Fury over Hair* (New York: David McKay, 1971), 23.

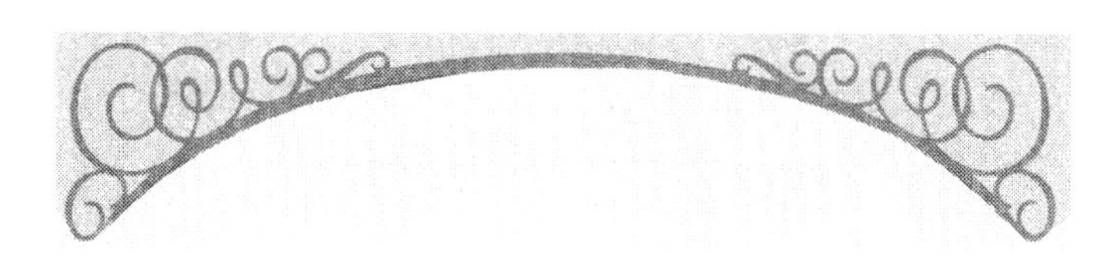

2 – How the Body Is Affected

The two verses that have stirred the hearts of many in these last days are found in I Corinthians 11, verse 15, ***But if a woman have long hair, it is a glory to her:*** and verse 10, ***For this cause ought the woman to have power on her head because of the angels***. Why? What is the confusion all about? Could the body of Christ really be affected if a woman cuts her hair? Are these passages some verses that Paul wrote just to upset the women in the church, or are these verses that have significance? Is it a cultural thing, or does it involve a deeper spiritual meaning?

Further in the same chapter, Paul wrote almost in the same breath about the importance of practicing communion. It's a paradox that, in every denomination, Christians will celebrate the Lord's Supper by taking communion but ignore the principle found in the women having long, uncut hair.

Hair Battle in the Body

It is amazing to see that many still wrestle with these few passages of Scripture. Why is there such a struggle with women's hair length today? What possibly could be the significance? Is it simply an obedience issue, or does God have a plan for His women in these last days?

As we near the end times, needing the power of the Lord like never before, I marvel that the women who used to uphold this biblical hair principle with long flowing tresses now no longer think it is important. Who has changed: the Bible or these women? The coming of the Lord is so soon we don't have time to question the validity of God's Word, but we need to trust that He put these verses of Scripture there for a reason. However, that is not good enough for some. By exploring each aspect through many examples, we are able to plainly come up with some concrete answers.

This hair length controversy is bringing many changes in churches today. These swift changes usher confusion to one's mind. Grievously, many are asking, "What's happening to us? Why are our power and glory slipping away from the church?" Perhaps, it's because we don't understand that the blessings of God come in our lives from our obedience to His Word.

As you ponder the perplexing problem of hair length, you can't help asking questions: Do God's women no longer wish to carry their symbol of submission to authority? Don't they care that long, uncut hair is a glory to them and to have short hair is a shame according to the Bible? Have they forgotten that the angels are watching to see if they have this mark of distinction? Can't they remember that this was God's original method of affirming the difference between male and female?

Even though the Scriptures can answer a number of these questions, there are those Christians who just choose to ignore it. The Word of God supports these truths, but some no longer feel it is valid in their lifestyle or actions. Many saints are feeling the effects of the dispute. And some churches have quit preaching on the subject altogether, believing that it doesn't matter any more.

Can this affect the body of Christ as a whole? Do we think our opponent, the world, doesn't notice us any more? Of course, the answers to these two questions are, quite frankly, yes. Yes, this does affect the body of Christ as a whole. Yes, the world still does notice us. To give you a recent example, a sister in the Lord told me that she wore her waist-length hair down at work the other day. When she went into the break room, some of her coworkers commented on how beautiful her hair was. She later got to witness to them and tell of her conviction; *they still notice!* The spirit of unity in the church is also in danger of survival and could be totally destroyed.

Endangered Unity

First of all, when ladies in the body of Christ go against God's Word and cut their hair, the unfortunate result is extreme disunity. The Holy Ghost cannot flow through hearts that are full of partiality. The ***unity of the Spirit in the bond of peace*** is stifled when everyone is looking over each other's shoulders, full of different opinions. Some believe that there is much significance to the principle of women's hair, others believe trimming hair is okay if you just keep it long, and others think that if you are not allowed to cut your hair as you wish, you are in bondage. Jesus prayed for unity to be among His disciples in John 17:20-22:

> ***Neither pray I for these alone, but for them also which shall believe on me through their word; that they all may be one; as thou, Father, art in me, and I in thee, that they also may be one in us: that the world may believe that thou hast sent me. And the glory which thou gavest me I have given them; that they may be one, even as we are one.***

Such great strength, power, and effectiveness are in unity and oneness of spirit. The familiar story of the Tower of Babel found in the Book of Genesis illustrates this point. The people had a "who cares" attitude. They rebelled against God and His Word. This was the beginning of the self-religion called humanism. They might have thought, *We don't need God; we can do it on our own.* They were out to make a name for themselves. Perhaps the intent was to impress the inhabitants of the land of Shinar.

Their goal was to unite all the people into one kingdom. God was not ignorant; He knew exactly what was going on. He is truly just and fair in all His proceedings against sin and sinners. He apparently allowed them to proceed a good way in their enterprise before He put a stop to it, possibly so that they might have space to repent. When enough was enough, the Lord came down and said, ***Behold, the people is one, and they have all one language; and this they begin to do: and now nothing will be restrained from them, which they have imagined to do*** (Genesis 11:6).

Why was nothing restrained from them? They could accomplish what they set out to do because they had a unified effort. God is teaching in this verse a lesson in unity, whether the unified effort is for good or for evil. It took confusion to scatter these people and thwart their completing what they purposed in their heart to accomplish.

Women do not realize that cutting or trimming their hair has great significance that can cause severe confusion in the spiritual realm.

Confusion scatters the spirit of unity. We, the church, have set out to usher sinners into the presence of the Lord Jesus Christ, but confusion has stifled our efforts. Thus, the evangelistic attempts become futile.

There is another reason the commandment of unity in the church given by Jesus cannot be fulfilled. The reason is "a party spirit," explains Rev. Daniel Segraves, Executive Vice-President and Chairman of the Department of Theology of Christian Life College, in his book, *Hair Length in the Bible*. Segraves writes that a party spirit is usually "divided into numerous splinter groups."[1]

This term "party spirit" so adequately describes a disturbing dream I had one night. I dreamed that when I went into the church, it was like being at a big party. People were coming and going. There were several splinter groups off doing their own thing. Nobody was worshiping or praising the Lord, but everyone was laughing and talking. *This isn't what church is supposed to be like,* I thought in the dream. I looked around, and each person was mingling with different groups of people. Segraves's description made the meaning so clear. Think about it for a moment. When you're at a party, you are not unified but usually mingling from one group to the next.

Of course, one realizes that it wouldn't be that sinners who come to visit the church would recognize only whose hair is cut or uncut. Additionally, they should sense the feeling of "our oneness of spirit and purpose, a oneness that results in good works, which in turn gives glory to God,"[2] says Segraves. Disunity sabotages ***the power that worketh in us*** (Ephesians 3:20).

Power Source Threatened

Another lamentable result dishonoring the head causes in the church, maybe without our knowing it, is that it short-circuits one of the God-given power sources. Sometimes I wonder why the power of God is missing in our altar services. Is our power cut off from God? Could this be why, when we lay hands on the sick, they do not recover miracu-

---

1. Daniel Segraves, *Hair Length in the Bible* (Hazelwood: Word Aflame Press, 1989), 14.
2. Ibid.

lously or when we lay hands on the blind, they do not receive their sight? Jesus gave his disciples the ***power to heal sickness, and to cast out devils*** (Mark 3:15). As a church, we, too, should have this power, but how can we obtain it?

It may be obtained it through the act of obedience; however, by the mere snip of the shears, our power has been cut off and now lies dormant in the body of Christ. Hence, the sick, the lame, the blind go away disappointed and frustrated. Sure, the Lord fills those hungry souls with the Holy Ghost power by His mercy and grace, but we don't see the miraculous, wonder-working power of old! Keynote speaker Marietta Wolfe said at a Washington ladies' meeting, "The reason there is so little power and glory in some churches is because the ladies have so little power and glory on their heads!"[3]

The veil was the power, honor, and dignity of the woman in Oriental lands. Our veil is our uncut, consecrated hair. According to Revs. Archibald Robertson and Alfred Plummer in their book, *A Critical and Exegetical Commentary on the First Epistle of Saint Paul to the Corinthians*, "With the veil on her head she can go anywhere in security and profound respect. She is not seen; it is a mark of thoroughly bad manners to observe a veiled woman on the street. She is alone. The rest of the people around are nonexistent to her, as she is to them. She is supreme in the crowd. . . . But without the veil the woman is a thing of naught, whom any one may insult. . . . A woman's authority and dignity vanish along with the all-covering veil that she discards."[4]

Peter Lorie quotes in his book, *Superstitions*, a man by the name of Eric Maple, who states in his own book, *Superstitions and the Superstitious*, "The length of hair 'is merely a twentieth-century contradictory superstition which asks us to believe that the strength of the state and the stability of society generally is in some unexplained way dependent

---

3. Nona Freeman, "Endangered Glory," *Gospel Tidings*, 5.

4. Archibald Robertson, DD, LLD, and Alfred Plummer, MA, DD, *A Critical and Exegetical Commentary on the First Epistle of Saint Paul to the Corinthians*, 2nd ed. (1911; New York: Charles Scribner's Sons), 232.

upon the length of hair worn by its citizens.' "[5]

Hence, we can look back at the turn of the twentieth century, when not many women cut their hair. Before that time were recorded miracles, signs, and wonders. Charles Finney alone in his day won over one million souls to Jesus. The anointed evangelist, Mrs. Mary Woodworth Etter, saw hundreds come to Jesus Christ in her ministry from the year 1844 to 1916.[6]

But nowadays if you are a lady with long hair, you tend to stick out like a sore thumb and often have to give a reason for having it long. Many do not understand the biblical connection between the power and the hair because in the last eight decades women have freely cut it off with no recourse. (More about that in chapter five.)

How can we know for sure that there is a connection between miracle-working power and the power on the woman's head? Let's have a closer look at the verse of Scripture, I Corinthians 11:10, ***For this cause ought the woman to have POWER*** [emphasis mine] ***on her head because of the angels.***

The word "power" comes from the Greek word *exousia* that is defined as: authority, jurisdiction, liberty, privilege; force; capacity (*Strong's Concordance* #1849). The passage we find in Luke 10:19 also uses the same word, "power," ***Behold, I give unto you POWER*** [emphasis mine] ***to tread on serpents and scorpions, and over all the power of the enemy: and nothing shall by any means hurt you***.

Although the word "power" is used twice in Luke 10:19, two different words are used in the original Greek. The verse is better rendered ***Behold, I give unto you AUTHORITY, or I give unto you the JURISDICTION or CAPACITY to tread on serpents and scorpions***. Any of the definitions above could be inserted.

The "power of the enemy"simply means the force or miraculous power by which the devil manifests his wickedness. In speaking of "ser-

5. Eric Maple, "Hair-length and its associations," *Superstitions and the Superstitious*, rpt. in Peter Lorie, *Superstitions* (New York: Labyrinth Publishing), 48.

6. *Miracles, Signs and Wonders Wrought in the Ministry of Mary Woodworth Etter* (Portland: Apostolic Bible Publishers, 1984).

pents and scorpions," Jesus was talking about the power of the devil—demons, evil spirits, and all his cohorts. We need to remember that Holy Ghost-filled women and men have authority over the devil and all his entourage! Of course, God Himself is the power behind our authority.

Another example of power distribution is mentioned in Matthew 10:1, ***He gave them POWER*** [emphasis mine] ***against unclean spirits, to cast them out, and to heal all manner of sickness and all manner of disease.***

Policemen who direct traffic during the rush hour just raise their hands to stop the cars. Do these men have the physical power to stop vehicles if the drivers choose not to stop? No. The police use their authority that is vested in their badges granted to them by the government they serve.

Another example of "exousia-power" is when Jesus referred to the power that would raise Him from the dead (John 10:18). Also, in Matthew 9:6, the Bible says that Jesus ***hath power on earth to forgive sins***. His awesome power is given to those ladies who choose to wear their hair long and uncut. The source of power comes in submission to this truth in God's Word!

Indian scalping enemy

Cooper points out that the "Sioux Indians accepted hair so much as the seat of strength that they scalped their enemies to take away their power even in death."[7]

Dr. Herman Goodman, noted physician and author, informs that the "natives of Amboyna thought their strength would desert them if they were shorn."[8] "Many Cambodians," Goodman adds, "consider it a grave offense to touch a person's head."[9]

---

7. Cooper, 41.

8. Herman Goodman, BS, MD, *Your Hair, Its Health, Beauty, and Growth* (New York: Emerson Books, 1950), 255.

9. Ibid., 254.

Glory Diminished

What about the significance in I Corinthians 11:15, where it says that the woman's hair is a ***glory to her***? ***But if a woman have long hair, it is a glory to her: for her hair is given her for a covering.***

This word "glory" in Greek, *doxa*, was used 145 times alone in the New Testament. One example of "glory" is when Jesus described Solomon, ***in all his glory*** (Luke 12:27). Solomon had remarkable power, prosperity, and glory. He took full advantage of the favorable conditions for trade expansion both by land and by sea. His main source of wealth came from his copper mining and refining. He built cities for his chariots and horsemen, as recorded in I Kings 9:19. The city had stables for at least forty-five thousand horses.

Three women c. 1900

The news of this man's glory and power reached so far south that the Queen of Sheba had to come to see for herself. To her amazement, she left that place saying, ***The half was not told me*** (I Kings 10:7).

The *American Dictionary* and the *Webster's Dictionary* both define "glory" as: 1. A great honor, praise, or distinction given by common consent. 2. Something that brings honor or renown. 3. A highly praiseworthy asset, esp. a physical asset, as beautiful hair! It's interesting that these two dictionaries use beautiful hair for an example of glory.

In researching, I found that Charles Darwin, in his writings, *The Origin of Species by Means of Natural Selection—The Descent of Man and Selection in Relation to Sex*, quoted the apostle Paul from I Corinthians 11:15, that a woman's hair is her glory.

Darwin, the archenemy of creation truth, stated that "long tresses are now and were formerly much admired as may be observed in the works of almost every poet."[10] This is demonstrated in the poem by the English Cavalier Robert Herrick to his lover Julia, whose hair was bundled in a golden net:

> Tell me, what needs those rich deceits,
> Those golden Toyles, and Trammel-nets,
> To take thine haires when they are knowne
> Already tame, and all thine oune?
> 'Tis I am wild, and more than haires
> Deserve these Meshes and those snares.
> Set free thy Tresses, let them flow
> As aires doe breathe, or winds doe blow.[11]

"The power of a woman's hair," states Goodman, "was used to ensnare and enchain the hearts of men."[12] Just about everywhere in the world, women's hair has been an object of sexual attraction. Its potentially seductive power has gone into mythology with the story of the Lorelei, who sang on a rock overlooking the Rhine while combing her long, golden tresses, luring to their deaths unwise boatmen who raised their eyes.[13]

Henry Wadsworth Longfellow wrote, in *The Saga of King Olaf*:

> Not ten yoke of oxen
> Have the power to draw us
> Like a woman's hair.[14]

Smithsonian Institution's book on hair states, "Long hair was considered so vital to the royal Frankish right of succession that in the

---

10. Charles Darwin, *the Origin of Species by Means of Natural Selection—The Descent of Man and Selection in Relation to Sex* (1859; Chicago: William Benton, 1952), 588.
11. Cooper, 73.
12. Goodman, 251.
13. Cooper, 68.
14. Henry Davidoff (ed.), "Hair," *Pocket Book of Quotations* (1942; New York: Pocket Books, 1952), 127.

sixth century AD Queen Clotilde allowed her grandchildren to be murdered rather than shorn."[15] "A means of extracting confessions from prisoners at the bar in old Dutch courts," declares Goodman, "was to threaten cutting the hair. Usually the prisoner made a full confession at that threat, after the most painful means of torture had yielded nothing."[16]

The Smithsonian researchers said further, "The *Ladies' Dictionary of 1694* stated gracefully, 'Indeed the Hair is a very Great Ornament.' A century earlier, Martin Luther admitted, 'The hair is the finest ornament women have.' "[17]

Seven Sutherland Sisters c. 1880

America was entranced during the 1880s with the seven Sutherland sisters, who traveled with the great Barnum and Bailey Circus. The show had the billing, "The Longest Hair in the World." The total length of hair that flowed over the backs of these sisters was a staggering thirty-six feet, ten inches. The last of the Sutherland sisters, Grace, died January 19, 1946.[18]

The girls were the daughters of Fletcher Sutherland, an upstate New York farmer who also worked as a part-time lawyer and preacher. Later, they earned a small fortune by lending their names to a hair tonic company. Soon, women all over agreed with their popular advertising slogan: "A Woman's Crowning Glory Is Her Hair."[19]

---

15. Smithsonian Institution's National Museum of Design, *Hair* (New York: M. H. Birge & Sons Co., 1980), 8.
16. Goodman, 255.
17. Smithsonian, 25.
18. John Durant and Alice Durant, *Pictorial History of the American Circus* (New York: A. S. Barnes and Company, 1957), 121.
19. Severn, 114-115.

Just a few of the many, many examples in history will prove that the world at one time believed that women's hair was a glorious thing to behold. It's a wonder that anyone would want to cut it off! However, in the mid-1990s [the time of this book's first printing], there are many reasons why women do. Some personal reasons I've heard consist of the following: 1) She has low self-esteem, 2) It's easier to take care of, 3) She didn't like the manner in which this hair principle was preached or presented to her, 4) She has a direct rebellion-problem toward God, 5) She thinks she is taking a "Nazarite vow," 6) She says she "just doesn't have a conviction about it," 7) She just wants to cut off the dead or split ends, 8) She says, "I'm not cutting my hair; I'm just trimming the bangs," and finally, 9) She just wants to have the feeling of control in some part of her life.

If these reasons were not originally there when she first was converted, what actually happened? Did she lose sight of the heavenly goal? Maybe she doesn't understand the total significance. Could it be that she changed her mind, then drifted from God, or vice versa? She, perhaps, forgot how God was transforming her life.

Holy Ghost Transformation

It is an interesting phenomenon that after a woman fully repents of her sins, has been obedient to water baptism, and is later filled with the Holy Ghost, she then becomes a beautifully transformed woman.

Shortly thereafter, God begins to deal with her about her hair, clothes, attitudes, and other areas of her life. When she becomes a new creature in Jesus Christ, He begins to mold her and make her into a godly woman. Her desire to be submissive to Christ becomes stronger and stronger. She begins to learn about prayer, fasting, fellowship, and the other exciting challenges of serving the Lord.

One may notice that as her spirit begins to soften, she becomes more sensitive to the Lord and others around her. She begins to dress modestly and stops cutting her hair. The new babe in the Lord decides to let it grow as a sign of submission unto God and His Word. I've witnessed this often in many new believers. I know this to be true personally because it happened to me . . . and numerous other women I've known since being in the church.

However, during this transforming process, the most disheartening thing happens. As time goes on—and it may be months, years, or whatever—the Lord may try to perfect her more and more by sending some trials her way. She begins to struggle and weakens in faith. In many cases, her heart is hardened and she is not prayed up, so she inevitably slips back, trying to adjust the outer person without dealing with the inner person.

Consequently, after the dust is settled, she finds her way back to the altar with her hair trimmed or, worse still, cut off completely. What gut-wrenching effects does this have on the others around her? And why is it such a big disappointment to the members in the body of Christ? Let me try to explain it by telling you a personal experience.

How the Body's Affected

One of my longtime friends in church went through a time of testing. I knew the trials she went through had been hard, but I didn't know how it made her waver. One day I noticed her at the altar with her hair cut short. At first when I saw it, I couldn't believe that her hip-length hair was whacked off at least eighteen inches. I thought that I was seeing things. I didn't want to judge, but it was very noticeable. It was as if a knife was stabbed into my heart. I grieved so hard it was like a death. *Why would she do that?* I thought. I had to talk to her to let her know what I was feeling, but she gave me no real concrete answer.

She had that beautiful hair you'd admire so much. You know, the kind that is thick, long, and gorgeous. Was her faith really shaken enough to make her respond in drastic measures? After we were finished praying I had a chance to tell her that I was feeling so disappointed. We'd been friends for a long time and had been through a lot together. It felt to me that when she cut her hair off, it was as if she cut my hair, too!

How could this be? Was I just overreacting? No. Then why would I take this so personally? After praying about it, the Lord showed me it was because the Bible says we are all part of the body of Christ. In the Book of Romans, the two verses of Scripture that had the most impact on me were:

So we, being many, are one body in Christ, and every one members one of another (Romans 12:5).

For none of us liveth to himself, and no man dieth to himself (Romans 14:7). (Also see I Corinthians 10:17; 12:12; Galatians 3:28.)

I liken it to someone breaking an arm or a leg. His physical body will be in great pain. He will limp for some time, causing the body to slow down, or may even have to learn how to write with the hand opposite from the one he broke. It has the same result when a sister cuts off her glory. There is a cause and effect. The spiritual body cannot help but be affected in the same way.

Just recently my pastor, Jim Shoemake, preached a message that so adequately iterates the point. He reminded us about the story of Achan, found in the Book of Joshua, chapter seven. The tragedy of Achan's story is that this man did not realize the severe ramifications of his actions.

The things he stole were not necessarily bad. The goodly Babylonish garment, the shekels of silver, and the wedge of gold—these things were, in and of themselves, harmless, but God wanted these things consecrated to Himself. Achan no doubt justified having them.

His selfish motives were mere lust and covetousness, only to discover that he later had to hide all his stolen possessions. The result was the coveted treasures ended up being worthless to him. Instead he reaped humiliation and capital punishment.

His punishment was drastic. Achan was not alone in his sin. He did not just hurt himself. The whole nation of Israel suffered the embarrassment of defeat in the battle of Ai. The effects of Achan's sin hit his family also. The Bible states that all his family suffered; his sons, his daughters, his oxen, his asses, his sheep, his tent, and all that he had were destroyed also (Joshua 7:24-26). Therefore, we can conclude that this story teaches us the serious effects of disobedience and the consequences of sin. The results will affect everyone.

With that story in mind, my pastor adamantly declared, "There are very few actions that we can get involved in that do not affect someone else. It's a rare chance for any of us to be involved in something that will not affect somebody else." My friend who flopped through her trial needed to understand that she first followed the spiritual principle of obedience when she got saved. Under submission she allowed her hair to grow as unto the Lord. At a moment of weakness, she broke a spiritual principle by her disobedience to God's commands. This type of sin, like all sin, needs to be repented of.

Later, I noticed that a few more ladies had cut their hair. It seemed to send a rippling effect to some of the members of the congregation just as if a stone were cast in a lake. All because of one? I can't say for sure, but perhaps a spirit tried to come in and take control. Someone may say you shouldn't be influenced by someone else's sin but stay strong. This may be true, but look how Achan's failure penalized all of Israel. They suffered a great defeat at the battle of Ai. It's best to be obedient to the Lord's commands at all times no matter what trial may come your way.

If we love the Lord, we'll keep His commandments (John 14:15). The Word of God declares in I John 2:4, ***He that saith, I know him, and keepeth not his commandments, is a liar, and the truth is not in him***. The Lord loves us. He cares about what we do. He wants to guide and to watch over us. He gave His angels charge over us to keep us in all our ways.

Maybe some still have a hard time understanding that there are certain basic truths in the Word of God for Christians to follow. The apostle Paul was not merely restricting women in taking care of their appearance but was also resolving the grooming confusion for both the woman and the man.

With this understanding, we discern that disobedience to His principles can cause the unity of the body of Christ to be endangered and our power source threatened. If the ladies are free to do as they please, the glory of the church will diminish completely. And, perhaps, this is why the glory is absent altogether in some churches today.

My endeavor is to help those struggling with this matter to comprehend its importance. My goal is to benefit and not to badger. ***When wisdom entereth into thine heart, and knowledge is pleasant unto thy soul; discretion shall preserve thee, understanding shall keep thee*** (Proverbs 2:10-11).

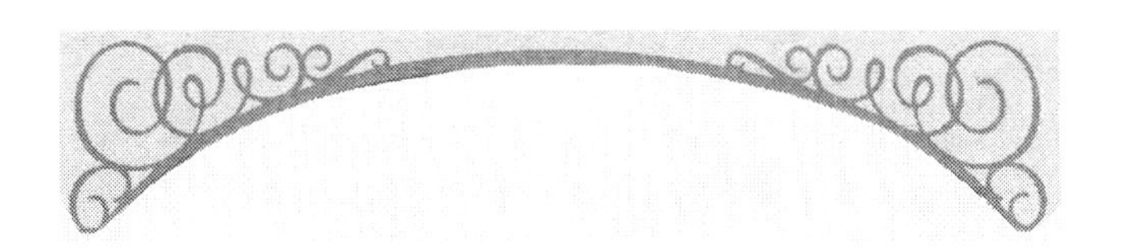

3 – Biblical Aspects

The Lord cares about us and what we do. Our Christianity cannot be without the Lord leading us as we learn to walk in the Spirit. What comfort we have in knowing that He watches over us and guides us! According to Psalm 91:11, He gives ***his angels charge over thee, to keep thee in all thy ways***. Many women forget that the angels are presently watching over us. They especially watch over those women who wear their long, uncut hair as a sign of submission.

Angelic Audience

How can we know for sure that the angels are watching? Although many people believe in the presence of angels, let's look again in the Bible to read what it says about the angels. According to David, king of Israel, in Psalm 34:7, ***The angel of the LORD encampeth round about them that fear him, and delivereth them***. In the Book of Ecclesiastes, we read that King Solomon further cautioned us not to revoke vows that we have confessed to our angel: ***Suffer not thy mouth to cause thy flesh to sin; neither say thou before the angel, that it was an error*** (Ecclesiastes 5:6).

And the apostle Paul in the New Testament declared reflectively, ***For we are made a spectacle unto the world, and to angels, and to men*** (I Corinthians 4:9). When he said that, the gladiatorial contests may have been fresh on his mind. He pictured all the world, even God's angels looking on while we walk with the Lord here on earth. Not only do angels look on, but they also minister to those who shall be heirs of salvation: Hebrews 1:14, ***Are they not all ministering spirits, sent forth to minister for them who shall be heirs of salvation?***

It is evident from the previous passages of Scripture that the angels are invisibly present about us always. In earlier times, people freely accepted the existence of angels. Jewish people retold the ancient stories of how angels assisted Abraham, Moses, Elijah, Balaam, and Daniel.

The New Testament also records letters that warn against the common practice of angel worship. The Bible speaks of the angels standing by with a desire to look into our salvation (I Peter 1:12). In the Book of Isaiah, chapter 14, we read in verse 12 about the pride of Satan and his angels that caused them to be ***cut down to the ground***; thence, they were all stripped of their prestigious positions. For further study, see Ezekiel 28; Jude 1:6; and II Peter 2:4.

Loretta and David Bernard, authors of *In Search of Holiness*, say the woman must have power on her head as a mark, a sign because of the angels. They further state, "She [the woman] is to be an example even to angels. They are looking to see if she has the mark of consecration, submission and power with God, or if she is rebellious like Satan."[1] "The woman is a type of the church," Bernard and Bernard conclude, ". . . and she signifies to the angels whether or not the church is being submissive to Christ, the head of the church."[2]

In the popular tract, "For Ladies Only," written by M. J. Wolff, "Paul's writing '***because of the angels***' (verse 10) proves, without doubt, that the subjects of women, long hair, and angels are connected with the subjects of obedience, example, and testimony."[3]

According to Dr. Matthew Black, the general editor of *Peake's Commentary on the Bible*, "if a woman is unveiled in prayer she has no protection against evil angelic forces, the spiritual plane which she has entered being dangerous; her veil would be her 'authority' against them."[4] If this is true, the enemy can see whether or not the lady has her covering on when she goes to prayer. If she does not, according to Black, the lady becomes open prey for the onslaught of evil. This happens in the physical realm or in the mind, where most spiritual battles are fought.

---

1. Loretta Bernard and David Bernard, *In Search of Holiness* (Hazelwood: Word Aflame Press, 1981), 131.
2. Ibid.
3. M. J. Wolff, "For Ladies Only," tract no. 107 (Hazelwood: Pentecostal Publishing House).
4. Matthew Black, DD, D.Litt., D.Theol., FBA (ed.), "The Scandal of Unveiled Women," *Peake's Commentary on the Bible* (Nelson, 1962), 838.

And to put this theory to the test, think of all the women whom you know who have knowingly rebelled against the hair principle and have chosen not to wear their "covering." Is her life better or worse? Is her life flourishing in the blessings of God, or is she struggling with multiple trials that constantly plague her? Do you think there could be a correlation between submission, obedience and blessings?

God Sent a Dream

I worked with a new convert for some time. She wrestled with the biblical hair principle. She would do well for a while, then cut her hair. Then she would pray, repent, and reconsecrate her life to God, but after a few months, she would cut her hair again. This was her cycle for years.

Then one day she told me that she prayed earnestly for God to speak to her about this hair thing and what the importance was. She said the Lord gave her the answer in a dream. This is what she told me. How true it is we may never know, but the Lord knows.

She dreamed she was in heaven. There was a bright light. She couldn't see the Lord, but she heard His voice. She looked to one side. She saw a huge number of angels standing there. She asked the Lord what these angels were for.

The Lord replied, "Those angels were created and are assigned strictly to those women who do not cut their hair," speaking of the consecrated, godly women. "They are to give these women power, protection, and provision," He said reassuringly. Then her dream ended.

Wow, that was quite a dream! I thought. The dream God sent her strengthens my conviction I already had. I rejoiced with her that the Lord had been gracious to reveal this to her. It helped her for a while. Soon time went by. Her problem, I realized, was more of a deep-seated rebellion problem. My heart was grieved for her. I hated to see anyone walk away from the Lord. Even though God spoke to her in a dream, this lady eventually stopped coming to our church.

Nazarites in the Nineties?

I have heard some say it's okay to trim their hair because they were taking a Nazarite vow. Later, I wondered if there was some significance to that correlation, or is it an idea someone concocted in her mind to further perpetuate the hair confusion? Is it possible to take a Nazarite vow in this day and age to be an effective Christian?

I began to look into the significance of the Nazarite vow and found that it was for those Israelites in the camp who had a deep hunger to draw close to God. This vow involved "a separation or a consecration" for a specific period (from thirty to ninety days) of special devotion to the Lord. Anyone among the Hebrew people could take this vow; there were no tribal restrictions as for the Levitical priest. Rich or poor, free or bond, male or female—all were allowed to become a Nazarite.

The three biblical examples given were Samson (Judges 13:7), Samuel (I Samuel 1:11), and John the Baptist (Matthew 11:18-19). All were chosen by their parents or God at birth and remained Nazarites throughout their lives.

Nazarites consisted of the average laypersons who lived within the Israelite community. Their separation was demonstrated by abstaining from worldly things in three outward signs. The Lord told Moses in Numbers 6:3 that the person should ***separate himself from wine and strong drink***.

Nelson's Illustrated Bible Dictionary says, "Once a person decided to make himself ***holy unto the LORD*** (Numbers 6:8) for some special service he then agreed to abstain from wine and other intoxicating drinks. This prohibition was so strict that it included grapes, grape juice, and raisins."[5]

Another restriction was the person would refuse to cut his hair, including shaving (Numbers 6:5). The purpose of the Nazarite's uncut hair was to serve as a visible sign of his consecration to the Lord (Numbers 6:7). "The hair was a mark of separation," explains Bernard and Bernard.[6] They write that it signifies "strength, perfection, and glory; the free growth of hair on the head represented the dedication of a person with his whole strength and power to God."[7] The *Illustrated Bible Dic-*

---

5. Herbert Lockyer, Sr. (ed.), "Nazarite," *Nelson's Illustrated Bible Dictionary* (Nashville: Thomas Nelson, 1986), 749.

6. Bernard and Bernard, 127.

7. Ibid.

tionary relates, "The hair was regarded as the seat of life."[8]

Unger reports, "The long uncut hair of the Nazarite was the symbol of strength and abundant vitality and was worn in honor of the Lord as a sign that he belonged to the Lord, and dedicated himself to his service with all his vital powers. Then, too, a luxurious growth of long hair was looked upon as an ornament, and in the case of the Nazarite, was the diadem of the head consecrated to God."[9] (Compare Jeremiah 7:29.)

This method of consecration was not limited to the Hebrews. Their heathen neighbors also practiced this ritual. "In customs of other ancient nations," writes James E. Freeman, in *Manners and Customs of the Bible*, ". . . the Egyptians, Syrians, Greeks, Romans, and Arabs, it was customary in times of impending peril to consecrate the hair and beard to the gods."[10]

In 247 BC the Egyptian queen Berenice gave her hair on Aphrodite's altar for the safety in war of her brother-husband, Ptolemy III; her shorn locks, many during that day, were believed to be carried into the heavens and became the constellation Coma Berenices.[11]

The Nazarites would not go near or touch a dead body because it would make them ceremonially unclean. They would not even bury their own relatives. If a person accidentally broke his Nazarite vow, he had to undergo a ceremony of restoration for cleansing (Numbers 6:9-12) and present his offerings to the priest. According to *Nelson's Illustrated Bible Dictionary*, "It was as if he were starting all over again and the days already served under the vow did not count."[12]

"The offerings of the Nazarite at the completion of the period of the vow," *New International Version Study Bible* explains, were "extensive, expensive and expressive of the spirit of total commitment to the Lord during this time of special devotion."[13] When the specified

8. Douglas, "Nazarite," 1063.

9. Unger, "Nazarite," 780.

10. James M. Freeman, AM, "Vows–Nazarites," *Manners and Customs of the Bible* (Plainfield: Logos International, 1972), 453.

11. Cooper, 66, and Barbara Walker, *Myths and Secrets*, 367-368.

12. Lockyer, 749.

13. Kenneth Barker (ed.), *NIV Study Bible*, study notes (Grand Rapids: Zondervan, 1985), 199.

time was completed, the Nazarite could appear before the priest for the ceremony of release.

After offering a male lamb for a burnt offering, he would offer a ewe lamb for a sin offering, followed by a ram for the peace offering. Next would be an offering with a basket of unleavened bread, cakes of fine flour mingled with oil, and wafers of unleavened bread anointed with oil. All sacrifices were completed with the prescribed meat offerings and drink offerings.

As the grand finale, the person would cut off his hair that was allowed to grow long and burn it on the altar. The priest took a piece of the ram, one cake, and one wafer, and put them in the hands of the Nazarite and offered a wave offering. Only then was the Nazarite fully released from his vow.

The *Harper's Bible Commentary* adds, "any commitment to the holy God of Israel, whether by a priest or a Nazarite, was to be taken with the utmost seriousness and discipline for it impinged on the holiness of the whole community."[14]

In the case of Samson, however, though he was a Nazarite from birth, he obviously did not have it deep in his heart. He constantly defied the Nazarite separation edicts through his fleshly appetites. He presumably drank at a special feast he prepared, which is recorded in Judges 14:10. Commentators assume this to be true because drinking wine was a common practice at all Ancient Near East feasts.

In verses 8 and 9 of Judges 14, we find an occasion where he handled a carcass by the road that made an infringement of the law. The last of the violations Samson did is the time he demanded his parents get him a wife of the Philistines. By repeatedly negating his vows of separation, he reaped dreadful results and ultimately died an ignominious death (Judges 16:25-30).

It is not necessary to take a Nazarite vow nowadays to be an effective Christian. We simply need to present our bodies ***a living sacrifice, holy, acceptable unto God, which is [our] reasonable service*** (Romans 12:1). The Bible says in II Corinthians 6:17, ***Wherefore come out from among them, and be ye separate, saith the Lord, and touch***

14. Mays, "Law for Preserving the Holiness of the Camp," 187.

not the unclean thing; and I will receive you. When the hair of Samson was cut, he became like any other man. When we ladies cut our hair, we, too, become like everyone else in the world. The will of the Lord is for us to be a separate people, not look like everyone else in the world. Our long hair is usually the first thing anyone notices, mostly because it's different!

The apostle Peter wrote, ***Dearly beloved, I beseech you as strangers and pilgrims, abstain from fleshly lusts, which war against the soul*** (I Peter 2:11).

With a better understanding of the Nazarite vow, we know there can't be a correlation between a woman who trims her hair today and those who took the ancient Nazarite vow. No part of Scripture can be found to link the two. Perhaps this is an idea the devil concocted to perpetuate the confusion.

However, we can hear the Word of God instructing us to be ***as obedient children, not fashioning yourselves according to the former lusts . . .*** (I Peter 1:14), and to ***put ye on the Lord Jesus Christ, and make not provision for the flesh, to fulfil the lusts thereof*** (Romans 13:14). The Christian life cannot be a thirty-day vow here and there, but it is a day-after-day commitment that should keep us until eternity.

Every Woman's Dream

Behold, thou art fair, my love; behold, thou art fair; thou hast doves' eyes within thy locks: thy hair is as a flock of goats, that appear from mount Gilead (Song of Solomon 4:1). Those were the words spoken by the love-intoxicated King Solomon to his new Shulamite bride. It's every woman's dream to be filled with her husband's words of adoration. That wedding night for the Shulamite woman was as a dream come true. Her husband was pouring out gracious words of love and affection to his bride, yet he did not fail to speak of her hair.

It is interesting that Solomon repeated the same compliment in chapter 6:5. What was he really saying when he compared her hair to a flock of goats that appeared from Mount Gilead? Was there any significance, or were they just ordinary words of lovesick gobbledegook? Why does this metaphor create a beautiful scene in the mind of its readers?

Solomon used words that were picturesque to help us view the image from afar. If we are familiar with Israel's landscape, we will visualize black goats against the paler background. In our mind's eye, we can imagine a flock of goats wending its way on the mountainside.[15] King Solomon might have viewed this frequently from a distance through a favorite palace window. The dark waves of the Shulamite's hair falling down her back reminded him of the graceful goats of Gilead. Her hair was likened to the valuable treasure of goats.

In Bible times, Hebrew shepherds treasured the goat because it was such a useful animal. The goats are mostly black with long, silky hair. Workers wove the hair into a type of rough cloth. Families drank the goat's milk that is sweet and more nutritious than cow's milk. It is ideal for making cheese. The skins of the goats were used to make bottles that transported water and wine.[16]

The Crown of Love c. 1875

Later in chapter 7:5, Solomon used a different simile describing her hair. He said, ***Thine head upon thee is like Carmel, and the hair of thine head like purple; the king is held in the galleries***. It was no accident that Solomon compared the Shulamite's hair to purple. Just as the lady's hair is the most valuable commodity on her body, purple dye was the most highly valued commodity within the nation of Israel.

In Ugarit, a city of the Canaanites, wool was often dyed this color.

15. Mays, "The Wasp," 526.
16. Lockyer, "Goat," 56.

Purple was a monopoly of the Phoenicians and its name derived from the source of the dye. The dye itself was obtained from a species of shellfish, the *murex trunculus*, found in the Mediterranean Sea.

According to Franz Delitzsch, author of *Iris: Studies in Colour and Talks about Flowers*, "The dye taken from these shellfish is not their blood, but the slimy secretion of a gland which they have in common with all snails. This secretion is not at finest red or violet, but whitish. When exposed, however, to the sunlight it begins to color like a photographic surface, and, passing through shades of yellow and green, settles into the purple color, which is a combination of red and violet light and this mixed color, having sometimes more of a blue, sometimes more of a red hue, is ineffaceable.[17]

"A total of 250,000 mollusks was required to make one ounce of the dye, which partly accounts for its great price. A mantle of the best purple of Tyre, such as the luxurious habits of the empire required, cost ten thousand sesterces; i.e., over five hundred dollars."[18] The cost of the mollusk dye was a lot more expensive than our common $1.49 Ritz dye.

The metaphor "held in the galleries" suggests that the Shulamite's lovely hair bound or enslaved Solomon to her.[19] If her hair was shaggy or shaved, she would not have been able to capture her husband's affection. The Shulamite woman had no doubt that her husband thought she was beautiful.

In the heart of every woman is a need to be affirmed of her husband's tender love. There is double pressure for the woman; she knows she is the glory of her husband and that she must take care of the glory on her head. Those ladies who cut their hair for the reason of low self-esteem might well be suffering from an acute drought of affection.

Who knows what would happen if their husbands would run their fingers ever so gently over their "glory" more often? It would reassure the wives that God's beauty shines through them. Maybe some of those women would be released from the temptation to cut their hair to feel more desirable to their husbands. That would be every woman's dream!

---

17. Unger, "Colors," 213.
18. Ibid.
19. Criswell, study notes, 776.

Complete in Him

However, the truth of the matter is whether our husbands gloat over us or not, our self-esteem does not come from a person or from other people's approval. At one time or another, all of us women suffer from low self-esteem or a poor self-image. Our esteem can only come from the Lord, for we are ***complete in him*** (Colossians 2:10). He accepted us as we are and made us worthy on the cross at Calvary.

Think of the single women who do not have husbands to validate their worth. There is a verse of encouragement to our single sisters, in Isaiah 54:5, ***Thy Maker is thine husband; the LORD of hosts is his name; and thy Redeemer the Holy One of Israel; The God of the whole earth shall he be called***.

Paul said in Romans 12:3 that we are not to think of ourselves more highly than we ought to think but to think soberly. The only "esteem" we should have, as instructed in the Scriptures, is for others and especially for those who minister the gospel. The Bible says in Philippians 2:3, ***Let nothing be done through strife or vainglory; but in lowliness of mind let each esteem other better than themselves***. And in I Thessalonians 5:13, ***Esteem them very highly in love for their work's sake. And be at peace among yourselves.***

Unfortunately, the "poor self-esteem" excuse won't hold weight when we stand before God. There is no such thing as justifiable disobedience to the principles of God's Word—but more about the relationship of hair and self-esteem in chapter eight.

My Husband, My Covering

In the same chapter, I Corinthians 11, Scripture says that a woman praying or prophesying with her head uncovered dishonors her head (verse 5). We may take this to mean: if she prays or prophesies with her hair "cut," according to Scripture, she dishonors her head. Her head is her husband according to I Corinthians 11:3. However, "her uncut hair," Bernard and Bernard report, "is a symbol of submission to authority."[20]

---

20. Bernard and Bernard, 131.

The *Jerome Biblical Commentary* states that the expression "dishonoring her head" may mean that it could "wound her feminine dignity" and/or "shames her husband publicly by repudiating the sign of female subjection. Her shame is that of the woman whose head has been shaved; an allusion perhaps to the shameful chastisement predicted by Isaiah 3:24, as well as to natural repugnance."[21]

According to Elizabeth Rice Handford, in her book, *Your Clothes Say It For You*, "God has made a marvelous provision for a woman, and that is the loving, wise, compassionate protection of her husband. If she will submit herself to her husband, then she is safe from the most virulent of Satan's attacks. . . . A wife ought to welcome her husband's protection. She receives it by submitting to him."[22]

In a reading by *The Biblical Almanac*, a story illustrates the influence and power that a woman has in her marriage and her environment, whether she realizes it or not. "The story says that a pious man once married a pious woman. They were childless, so they eventually agreed to divorce one another. The husband then married a wicked woman and she made him wicked. The pious woman married a wicked man and made him righteous."[23]

The Bride's Glory

Marriage was indeed the most momentous event in the life of a Jewish person. The wedding ceremony began with a blessing proceeded by a short formula, then the young girl was given to her husband. The couple was ushered into a bridal chamber, where a canopy, named *huppah*, was prepared.

Usually betrothed women had to hide their hair and keep their heads covered. But at the moment she neared the nuptial couch, the girl

---

21. "The Traditions," *Jerome Biblical Commentary* (Englewood Cliffs, NJ: Prentice-Hall, 1968), 270.

22. Elizabeth Rice Handford, *Your Clothes Say It For You* (Murfreesboro, TN: Sword of the Lord Publishers, 1976), 60-61.

23. James I. Packer, AM, D.Phil. (ed.), "Summary," *The Biblical Almanac* (Nashville: Thomas Nelson, 1980), 430.

loosed her hair.[24] Robertson and Plummer state, "In the Hebrew marriage ceremony, as it is celebrated in modern Palestine . . . the husband snatches off the bride's veil and throws it on his own shoulder, as a sign that he has assumed authority over her."[25]

The marriage was consummated through sexual union as the guests waited outside. Once that fact was announced, the wedding festivities continued, with guests dropping by for the wedding feast. Traditionally, the wedding celebration lasted for a week or two.

The truly joyous occasion was special for the family in that they knew there would be another Jewish home established. The family's desire is that it may be a "Bayit Ne'eman, a faithful Jewish home," says Ben M. Edidin, author of *Jewish Customs and Ceremonies*. "One Hebrew term for marriage," Edidin writes, "is *Kidushin*, meaning a holy, sacred event."[26] The Mosaic law clearly stated that an Israelite was never to marry a Canaanite (Deuteronomy 7:1-3). Perhaps the Israelite would "be constantly tempted to embrace the spouse's gods," informs *Nelson's Illustrated Bible Dictionary*, thus, luring the loved one away from the one true God, Jehovah.[27]

In ancient times a man could easily obtain a divorce if his wife had the habit of loosing her hair. "There were sufficient reasons for divorce," affirms Meilsheim, ". . . any kind of misbehavior, unkindness to her husband's relatives in his presence, quarrelsomeness, that is to say talking to her husband so loudly that the neighbors could hear, spinning wool in the street, and if she had the habit of loosing her hair."[28]

In rabbinical literature, "The hair was regarded by the Rabbis as so powerful an augmentation of beauty that married women were recommended to hide it. In connection with this recommendation the Talmud relates the following: Kimhit, the mother of seven sons who successively held the office of high priest, was once asked by what merit of hers she was so blessed in her sons. 'Because,' said she, 'the beams of

---

24. Meilsheim, 84.
25. Robertson and Plummer, 233.
26. Ben M. Edidin, *Jewish Customs and Ceremonies* (New York: Hebrew, 1941), 63.
27. Lockyer, "Marriage," 681.
28. Meilsheim, 87.

my house have never seen my hair.' "[29]

One had to treat his or her marriage with honor and respect. The Israelite had to keep in mind the betrothal requirements accepted on the wedding day. Just as the women's hair in the ancient Jewish marriage had great significance, it still plays an important role for us today.

In using the ancient Jewish wedding ceremony as a metaphor, conference speaker, Rev. Lee Stoneking, on his tape, *The Pathway*, eloquently described the church preparing herself for the coming of the Lord.[30] Each aspect of the ceremony is portrayed in an analogy. During the message, Stoneking relates to his hearers the complex preparation process conducted by the betrothed maiden.

"She was thoroughly searched for intervening particles," explains Stoneking, "These are compared to sin in the life of the believer today." He states further that the law required her to visit the bathhouse before the wedding ceremony. She was to be totally immersed for cleansing. Her combed hair was to be worn down long and unbraided. No clips, no pins, nor anything else was allowed to be in it. Her hair must be in its purest form. The long hair was usually floating on top of the water then pushed down quickly by one of the handmaidens.

Stoneking begins to digress from his text into an in-depth explanation of the direct parallel between today's women of God who have long, uncut hair and the Jewish bride. The significance is rather eye-opening. "Preachers have miserably failed the women in the church today," confesses Stoneking, "by not helping them understand the vital and tremendous role they play in the kingdom of God." He declares emphatically, "Women have been chosen by God to do something that men can never do." He continues, "God in His wisdom has a plan to destroy the works of the devil that will be carried out by women."

He believes that the issue is not predominantly long hair itself, for numerous ladies everywhere have long hair. "In some cultures," he reminds us, "women's hair does not grow long." The reason for their hair not growing may be from the climate or their nutritional habits, but for whatever the reason, the real issue is whether the hair is cut or uncut.

---

29. Singer, "Rabbinical Literature," 158.
30. Lee Stoneking, *The Pathway*, tape.

Here in America, on the other hand, when a woman comes in the church, she expects her hair to grow out immediately yet many times has a hard time getting it to grow. That's because the hair has been ruined by being dyed, permed, crimped, heated, or bleached many times over.

By the time they come in, the scalp is injured and the roots are extremely damaged. The sisters in the Lord want it to grow out, but it can't. The results usually leave great frustration in the lives of the newly born-again woman. However, in spite of all the emotional turmoil, many ladies I know will have someone to anoint them with oil and pray for restoration of the hair growth. The Lord graciously replenishes the roots back to their normal state . . . and their glory begins to grow. We rejoice together that their hair begins to grow to the glory of God. It's a wonderful testimony!

"I don't understand it fully," admits Stoneking, "but I'm convinced that there is a direct connection with an angelic power and a woman allowing her hair to grow long" (i.e., not trimming at all). He has witnessed this over and over in his twenty-eight years of ministry. "There is an angelic presence found in their homes," Stoneking avows. "I know it; I've felt it!"

He capsulizes his point by stating that many times when he goes to a place where the women of God wear their hair long and uncut, he feels a sovereign presence. Just as he walks in the church and gets ready to preach, he says he can likewise feel the same deep, awesome, residential angelic power hovering over the congregation. "The glory," Stoneking claims, "is wonderful!" He has witnessed a tremendous move of God with healings, signs, wonders, and miracles. He declares that it is something powerful!

Nevertheless, in contrast, he also can sense the difference in those churches where the women do cut their hair or the women never hear it preached against. He has discovered that there is no real power present. Therefore, he concluded to say that he regretfully declines any invitations to preach at those churches any more.

The Jewish maiden had to keep herself pure for her bridegroom. We, as the bride of Christ, must keep ourselves pure and spotless from worldly things. Deception can creep in to lure the ladies from keeping their glory in the purest form. The pull to be like the world is strong, and the weak are ensnared by its deceiving lure.

This point was easily seen in the article that ran in the *Gospel Tidings* by author, missionary, and conference speaker, Nona Freeman. Serving God to her is "not a slavish devotion to fads and trends, but to be an example of godliness in this wicked world." She continues, "I have an intense desire to wash His feet with my tears of gratitude for His multitude of tender mercies and wipe them with my hair—so I'll handle my glory carefully—just in case."[31]

The Great Washing

When you think of an example of long, uncut hair in the New Testament, one immediately thinks of the two women in the Gospels who washed the feet of Jesus and dried them with their long hair. Jesus was deeply touched by their acts of worship, while the apostles were disturbed by these actions.

In Luke 7:38, we find the first woman, the nameless, penitent sinner who, no doubt, heard Jesus previously preach forgiveness from, perhaps, the edge of town. She was a woman of the city, a harlot who had an offensive reputation. However, that did not stop her. Abandoning her old life, she pushed her way through the crowd to get to the Pharisee's house where Jesus was.

At a moment's flash, fear gripped her tightly, for she knew that the law rigidly condemned harlots. The holy Scriptures declare in Deuteronomy 22:21 that all harlots must be stoned, and in Leviticus 21:9 they were to be burned.

Mary washing the feet of Jesus (Guido 1995)

31. Nona Freeman, 5.

Those good men present in the house could invoke either punishment on her . . . yet her remorseful heart ached within her. She had to see her Lord and Savior despite any accusing stares or leering glances.

Finally arriving at the door, she advanced boldly toward Jesus. With love and gratitude rapidly swelling in her soul, she took a deep breath and knelt behind him. She was in the presence of the holy God. His tender mercies and lovingkindness she felt became overwhelming.

The weight of her sinful life was ever so heavy upon her. . . . All she could do was sob uncontrollably. As tears poured down her cheeks and gently spilled on His feet, she kindly lifted one foot at a time to gently rub it.

When no more tears could be shed, she took her long, shamed glory in her hands and wiped His feet dry. The only way she knew to show her true love and affection was to kiss her Master's feet, for this man was like none other she'd met.

There was one thing left for her to do. She poured fragrant oil from her flask upon his feet, anointing him, as it were, with the oil of her gladness. Adoration, gratefulness, and thanksgiving shone in her tear-stained face.

The others never quite understood the love of the Master. Jesus forgave her sins and said her faith had saved her. She had a new chance at life. That glorious day was like no other; she could truly go in peace!

The second woman, recorded in John 12, was Mary of Bethany, sister of Lazarus, who anointed Jesus a week before His crucifixion. She knew in her spirit that His time was short. Her heart was full of appreciation for all the things He had done in her life. She was especially thankful to the Lord for raising her brother from the dead.

Mary used a jar of costly ointment to show her gratitude and adoration. The value of the ointment was three hundred pence (denarii), which is equivalent to a year's wages. The fragrance filled all the house, provoking unkind words about her extravagance.

Spikenard is an aromatic herb imported from the East. The precious ointment was used both to prepare bodies for burial and to consecrate kings. Anointing is usually done to the head, but Mary, in an act of utter humility, poured the ointment on His feet, then used her highest glory to wipe the lowest part of His body. Her tender expression indicates deep devotion to Jesus and her willingness to serve Him.

She remembered the day when her sister rebuked her for not helping in the kitchen. Jesus came to her rescue. "Mary chose that good part," Jesus said assuredly. Her sister, on the other hand, was engrossed in lavish entertainment. It seemed Martha was so used to Jesus coming over that she didn't have time any more to listen to the Master speak. Mary couldn't help but to drink in His every word. *One day,* she thought as she stared at His feet, *when I get an opportunity, I'll anoint Him king . . . king of my heart!*

Great appreciation and love were displayed by these two women in the Gospels. They washed the feet of Jesus and dried them with their long hair. They took advantage of an opportunity to worship the King of kings and Lord of lords. It was a dramatic demonstration. They were able to take their God-given glory and use it in an act of worship.

What a privilege! If their hair was shaved, trimmed, or cut short, they may not have had the opportunity to worship Jesus in such an unreserved way; . . . perhaps these stories would have never been recorded in the Bible. (See Appendix A for in-depth definitions of the words "shorn" and "shaven.")

In summary, we read from the Word of God that angels are presently watching over the body of Christ, especially women who have consecrated themselves unto the Lord and wear their hair long and uncut as a symbol of submission. We could believe, according to one woman's dream, that there are angels assigned to those of us who do not cut their hair. They will give us power, protection, and provision.

We know by our study of the Nazarite that we may not use this type of vow as an excuse to trim our hair. The Shulamite woman enthralled her husband-king by her beautiful, long, black hair. The two humble women of the New Testament who washed the feet of Jesus could have only done their acts of obeisance if their hair was kept long.

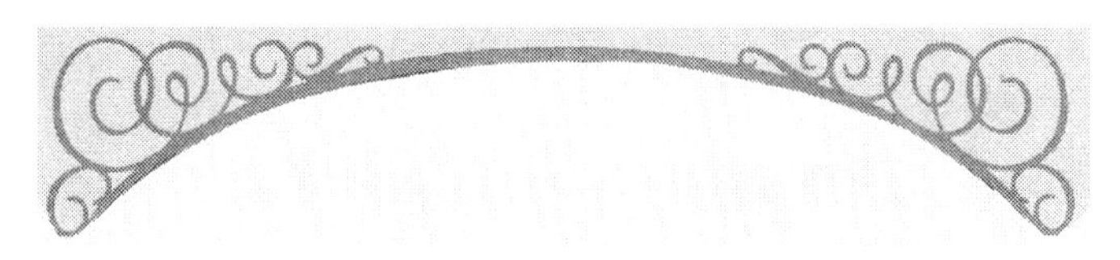

4 – Let History Speak

It wasn't an accident that God inspired Paul the apostle to write I Corinthians 11:14, 15, ***Doth not even nature itself teach you, that, if a man have long hair, it is a shame unto him? But if a woman have long hair, it is a glory to her***, and verse 10, ***For this cause ought the woman to have power on her head because of the angels***. What could have been the significance of these verses to the people whom Paul wrote? What were they like? Was their Corinthian society much different than ours today?

In the Days of Corinth

Although the meaning of these two verses are primarily based on spiritual principles, we can grasp a deeper understanding of what Paul the apostle was saying if we first take an in-depth look at the Corinthian people and their Greek culture. We will discover answers to the following questions: What was the spiritual condition of this city during the time this part of Scripture was written? How was immorality running rampant in the hearts of man? And what was it like to be a woman living in the city of Corinth?

Many of the passages the apostle Paul used in his two letters to the Corinthians show that he had an intimate knowledge of the people and their occupations. He was writing to a people who were wicked and steeped into hideous sin. They were very wealthy, well learned, and of prominent positions. By searching a little, you will discover that the Corinthian society was involved in ghastly lifestyles, yet its immorality wasn't too far removed from that of our day and country.

Every large city has its pocket of sin where prostitutes, strippers, gamblers, and drug dealers roam to get their fair share of the exchange of money. Tourists flock by to gawk at its disturbing sights. New York has Times Square; San Francisco has the North Beach district; New Orleans has Bourbon Street; and, of course, we can't forget Las Vegas and its sin-cursed streets. Iniquity is virtually everywhere in our nation.

The ancient world of Corinth was much the same; it had a despicable reputation. By our standards, we would think of its citizens as having a "wild" kind of lifestyle. The modern- day vernacular for the Greek verb, "to Corinthianize," was similar to the slang word we have today for someone who would shamelessly "cat around."

"Roman citizens made the Corinthians the butt of dirty jokes," reports the *New Student Bible*. "Playwrights consistently portrayed them as drunken brawlers."[1] It would be the last place anyone would want to start a church. However, to everyone's surprise after eighteen months of Paul's hard work, the church was founded and became one of the largest churches in the first century.

Several years later, he heard reports of the breakout of numerous spiritual ills. This is what prompted him to write the two letters to the Corinthians around AD 55. But just what exactly was going on?

Corinth had an estimated population that reached nearly seven hundred thousand during Paul's day. Four hundred thousand of them were slaves. The city had two very productive harbors, Cenchrea and Lechaeum. Although Corinth was not a university town like Athens, it was characterized by typical Greek culture. Their spiritual condition was far from knowing the one true God.

Its people were interested in Greek philosophy and placed a high premium on wisdom. This is what prompted the apostle to quote the prophet Isaiah, ***For it is written, I will destroy the wisdom of the wise, and will bring to nothing the understanding of the prudent*** (I Corinthians 1:19).

You can just imagine the apostle's stern face as he very provokingly asked, ***Where is the wise? where is the scribe? where is the disputer of this world? hath not God made foolish the wisdom of this world? For after that in the wisdom of God the world by wisdom knew not God, it pleased God by the foolishness of preaching to save them that believe*** (I Corinthians 1:20,21).

Then he wrote pointedly (verse 22), ***For the Jews require a sign,***

---

1. *New Student Bible*, notes by Philip Yancey and Tim Staffard (Grand Rapids: Zondervan, 1986), 1020.

and the Greeks seek after wisdom. He may have been thinking, *You have to understand this, folks,* as he continued writing verse 25, ***The foolishness of God is wiser than men***.

In other words, the Corinthians had to come to a place where they could not depend any more on their worldly wisdom but must trust in the Lord Jesus Christ. However, it was not easy for them to break away from trusting in their own abilities. How could they trust in a God they could not see? This was a practice they weren't accustomed to because of their generations of idolatrous worship.

The Greek Temples

There were more than twelve temples dedicated to their pagan gods in their small city. Special honor was made in the celebration festivals for their gods and goddesses. About one-fourth of a mile north was a temple of Asclepius, the god of healing. Located in the center of their city was the temple of Apollo, the sun god, head of all their other gods. In addition, they worshiped, among others, the gods of prophecy, music, medicine, and poetry.

The apostle Paul used a simile they could understand in the second book of Corinthians, ***And what agreement hath the temple of God with idols? for ye are the temple of the living God; as God hath said, I will dwell in them, and walk in them; and I will be their God, and they shall be my people*** (II Corinthians 6:16).

The most visited temple was built on the Acrocorinthus. This building was for the infamous goddess, Aphrodite, who was the patroness of prostitutes. The worship of this love goddess fostered prostitution in the name of religion. The city's two harbors would lure sailors and other travelers from all over the known world to come to indulge in its promiscuity.

At one time, there were over one thousand so-called sacred prostitutes who served the temple.[2] "Oftentimes," writes Donald Webster Cory in his book, *Homosexuality: A Cross Cultural Approach*, "the temple was filled with young people who had been taken as prisoners of

2. Ibid.

war and afterwards sold."[3] In many cases but not all, pagan priestess-prostitutes were owned by the temple itself while others rented a space to engage in their trade. According to Dr. Fernando Henriques, lecturer in social anthropology, Leeds University, in his book, *Prostitution and Society*, "For the ordinary citizen in quest of 'love' the brothels were the most convenient and cheapest method available."[4]

These temple servants openly worked their trade and with such success, according to the geographer Strabo, "the city owed its prosperity to the attraction of their entertainers."[5] "One of the reasons Corinth was such a rich city," state Bullough and Bullough, "was that thousands of strangers came there to visit the girls."[6] "Solon, the great Athenian lawgiver, was the founder of the city's brothel system."[7]

There were several levels of prostitutes, from the high-class hetaira, courtesans, dancers, and flute players to the impoverished streetwalker. All of them sold themselves for a mere demisere, which today would be equal to two cents.

"Prostitution was accepted as a natural way of life," Bullough and Bullough explain, "so much so that many states levied a tax on its practitioners."[8] The Greek states regulated the fees and kept track of them in order to collect the prostituted tax. Their cost was next to nothing, only an obol or a penny and a half. "The fees paid, low as they may be," expounds Henriques, "accrued to the state and were used partly for running expenses of the temple. The remainder was a profit to the state."[9]

My research efforts have led me to agree with *The Jerome Biblical Commentary*, "There is no evidence for the statement of some commentators that prostitutes in Greece shaved their heads. Rather, in the pursuit

---

3. Donald Webster Cory, *Homosexuality: A Cross Cultural Approach* (New York: Julian Press, 1956), 292.

4. Dr. Fernando Henriques, MA, *Prostitution and Society* (New York: The Citadel Press, 1962), 47.

5. Oscar Broneer, "Corinth Center of St. Paul's Missionary Work in Greece," *Biblical Archaeologist*, vol. 14 (1951), 88.

6. Vern Bullough and Bonnie Bullough, *Women and Prostitution: A Social History* (Buffalo: Prometheus Books, 1987), 39.

7. Henriques, 47.

8. Bullough and Bullough, 36.

9. Henriques, 49.

of their trade they took great pains with their coiffure."[10] The harlot of Greece knew the seductive power of the hair. In order to lure a prospect with anticipation and expectancy, she saw to it that hours were spent in dressing her tresses to win the attraction of some. And, in studying crime and punishments, I didn't find that shaving the head was a sentence for the crime of prostitution; instead, I found that the law of Moses gave the sentence for her to be ***burnt with fire*** (Leviticus 21:9) or to be stoned ***with stones that she die*** (Deuteronomy 22:21).

I did find Freeman stating in his book that for punishment they did "tear the hair out by the roots."[11] Nehemiah 13:25 says that he did this to the Jews, ***And I contended with them, and cursed them, and smote certain of them, and plucked off their hair. . . .*** "It is said that the ancient Athenians punished adulterers," Freeman continues, "by tearing the hair from the scalp and then covering the head with hot ashes."[12]

As you can tell, Corinth was a center for open, unbridled immorality. The apostle Paul had to admonish the Corinthians abruptly, ***Know ye not that your bodies are the members of Christ? shall I then take the members of Christ, and make them the members of an harlot? God forbid. What? know ye not that he which is joined to an harlot is one body? for two, saith he, shall be one flesh*** (I Corinthians 6:15, 16).

The apostle had to virtually retrain their way of thinking. Tolerating the idea of incest did not seem so terrible to its church members, so Paul had to write in I Corinthians 5:1, 2: ***It is reported commonly that there is fornication among you, and such fornication as is not so much as named among the Gentiles, that one should have his father's wife, and ye are puffed up, and have not rather mourned. . . .***

In other words, Paul received a report that there was sexual immorality among the members of the church that did not occur even with the pagans. Instead of having grief about it, they were arrogant!

As dreadful as it may seem, the Corinthians didn't stop at female prostitution or incest, but they were heavily involved with pederasty, a practice nowadays we would gasp at. This prurient practice was more than merely tolerated. It was, in fact, deeply admired.

10. *Jerome Biblical Commentary*, 270.
11. James M. Freeman, 198.
12. Ibid.

These catamites [young beautiful boys] lived in the temple, competing with the women to sell themselves to older men. However, most men had their own 'favorites,' whom they bought and kept until the boy reached the age of fifteen. Solon once said,

> You shall cherish a beautiful boy
> As long as he remains beardless.[13]

Immorality Increases

Cory records an article written by Hans Licht, who states, "Pedophilia was to the Greeks at first the most important way of bringing up the male young."[14] They were involved in the extensive trade in boys, chiefly bought by the Phoenician shipmasters to fill the harems of wealthy military officers.[15]

Greek literature, art, poetry, and mythology were saturated with its despicable idealism. Euripides, the negativist, gives enthusiastic expression recorded in the poem, *Opaidez*: "O what a magic comfort are boys to men!"[16]

Plutarch, a Greek biographer and philosopher who lived in Corinth at the time of Paul, wrote a story to expose the existence of the rape of boys. It's a story of a prominent man, Archias, who was well known among the Corinthians. He was in love with the most beautiful boy, Actaeon, son of Melissus. Since the boy refused to be persuaded, Archias resolved to rape him with violence. He consequently rode at the head of a number of friends and slaves before the house of Melissus and attempted to carry off the boy. But the father and his friends offered a bitter resistance, the neighbors also assisted, and during the struggle between the two parties, the lad was drug hither and thither, was fatally injured, and died.[17]

---

13. Cory, 351.
14. Ibid., 295.
15. Ibid., 304.
16. Ibid., 277.
17. Ibid., 309.

Greek love of boys

Robert Flaceliere informs,"No one would have thought the less of Pericles for making love to young boys. . . ."[18] Cory states, "The sensual love of the Greeks, was also directed towards their boys and that they sought and found in intercourse with them community with the soul."[19]

This practice however, was not strange to these Mid-Eastern lands. Israel was warned by God not to be involved with such abominable actions. Deuteronomy 23:17, 18 declares, ***There shall be no whore of the daughters of Israel, nor a sodomite of the sons of Israel. Thou shalt not bring the hire of a whore, or the price of a dog, into the house of the LORD thy God for any vow: for even both these are abomination unto the LORD thy God***. According to *The Illustrated Bible Dictionary*, "the contemptuous phrase 'dog' evidently refers to a male cult prostitute."[20]

In Rehoboam's reign, the business of male prostitution became a well-established practice (I Kings 14:24). The kings Asa, Jehoshaphat, and Josiah made active attempts to abolish this practice (I Kings 15:12; 22:46; II Kings 23:7).

It's no wonder the apostle Paul wrote in I Corinthians 6:9, ***Know ye not that the unrighteous shall not inherit the kingdom of God? Be not deceived: neither fornicators, nor idolaters, nor adulterers, nor effeminate, nor abusers of themselves with mankind. . . .***

These five evils took place in the temple of Aphrodite and virtually

---

18. Robert Flaceliere, *Daily Life in Greece at the Time of Pericles* (New York: MacMillan Company, 1968), 74.

19. Cory, 288.

20. Douglas, "Prostitution," vol. 3, 1289.

throughout the whole city. No doubt some new Christians, then, may have backslidden into these pagan practices again. Paul encouraged them not to be deceived by their modern-day thinking, which citizens thought to be normal. As reported by Henriques, "the brothel was regarded as a necessary means for preventing adultery."[21] "It is not hostile to marriage," Cory affirms, "but supplements it as an important factor in education."[22] Paul taught that the church was to remain untarnished by this perverted way of living.

The Greek Woman

In spite of all the prostitution going on, what did society think of women and marriage during this time? It is very obvious through the number of references given that the Greek culture was male-oriented and the woman's place obscured. In the ancient culture, the woman only came into the scheme of the Greek man as mother of his children and as manager of household matters.[23]

Proper women did not take part in public life. To the men of the time, it was inappropriate for a non-prostitute to make a public display of herself, to attract attention. Proper women did not accompany their husbands as guests to other houses, and if their husbands had dinner guests, wives were excluded from eating with them.

"Women did have some legal rights," explain Bullough and Bullough, ". . . they took part in making wills, in some family councils, and they had organizations of their own." But women were almost entirely dependent on the provision of their male relatives, husbands, fathers, brothers, or sons.[24]

Western Culture Compared

How can we compare their Greek culture to our Western world? In a nutshell, we in the western culture have a woman-centered culture.

---

21. Henriques, 48.
22. Cory, 298.
23. Ibid., 274.
24. Bullough and Bullough, 36.

By this, I mean though she is not the domineering factor, she carries much of the burdens of everyday life. Many times she is looked upon as a sex symbol or sex object. If she chooses to marry, she usually carries all the responsibility for wedding plans and expenses.

When child rearing comes into play, she is the primary caregiver, whether it be a single- or a double-parent home. When the kids go bad, people readily point the finger at the mom. If a single girl gets pregnant, the man usually walks off scot-free, abandoning all responsibility to the woman for the care and upbringing of that child. In many cases, the woman is more spiritually sensitive than the man and will carry the weight of prayer on herself. In his book, *Men: Some Assembly Required*, Chuck Snyder writes, "But in my opinion you as a woman have to carry more than your share of the burdens of the world, and life for you [ladies] may not seem much fun."[25]

This is not to cast stones at anyone but to help us realize what we Americans are facing in our culture. The pressures of womanhood are upon us ladies. It is not to bemoan the fact but to help us grasp the complexity of the woman's role. A thumbnail sketch of our western culture helps us see also that though it is woman-centered, it is still male-oriented.

Back to Paul's Day

When we read the verses in I Corinthians 11 on hair, we instantly want to direct the Scripture to the woman and put pressure on her to conform. Throughout history up to Paul's time and beyond, it was a fact of life that all women kept their hair long and untouched by scissors or any cutting devices.

According to lecturer in biblical studies at the University College of North Wales, Bangor, Margaret E. Thrall, in her commentary, *The First and Second Letters of Paul to the Corinthians*, "This was a disgrace for Greek women, and it was considered especially disgraceful

---

25. Chuck Snyder, "A Word from Chuck," *Men: Some Assembly Required* (Colorado Springs: Focus on the Family, 1995).

if they cut their hair off in order to imitate men."[26]

Long hair on men, however, was the practice throughout ancient Greece. According to Severn, "Greek men wore hair so long they had to braid it in top knots on the crowns of their heads and hold it in place with hairpins." Severn continues, "The brave Spartans spent hours combing out their long hair before they went out to battle."[27]

Achilles supposedly had such a beautiful, long head of hair it was likened to his bravery in the Trojan Wars. The strong man Hercules was pictured as having the long hair of a bull, and Homer, the Greek epic poet, called the Greeks "the long-haired ones."[28]

"At this period, civilized [decent] men, whether Jews, Greeks, or Romans, wore their hair short [and] . . . long hair was a permanent endowment of a woman, to serve as an enveloping mantle."[29] If you keep in mind the immoral lifestyles practiced by men during Paul's day and the fact that the women naturally kept their hair long, you'll suddenly realize the apostle Paul wasn't addressing women to keep their hair long as much as he was speaking to the men to keep their hair short. This was due to the torrent of homosexuality and effeminate actions of its citizens. According to the *Harper's Bible Dictionary*, short hair on men would alleviate any suspicion of effeminacy or homosexuality.[30]

Thus, the apostle was instructing his church brothers not to copy the worldly, effeminate pederasts but to look like holy, true men of God, walking in the image of Christ. By understanding the Greek culture at the time of Paul, we can now obtain a clearer picture of why the issue of hair in I Corinthians 11 was even addressed.

The Early Church Fathers

In this historical chapter, the significance of Scripture is revealed in a brighter light, strongly supported by the facts about the Corinthian

26. Margaret E. Thrall, *The First and Second Letters of Paul to the Corinthians* (Cambridge: University Press, 1965), 81.
27. Severn, 24.
28. Ibid.
29. Robertson and Plummer, 235.
30. Paul J. Achtemeier (ed.), *Harper's Bible Dictionary* (San Francisco: Harper & Row, 1985), 1183.

citizens. But did it stop in Paul's day, or was a continuous struggle waged throughout the ages to keep the hair on one's head in accordance with Scripture? Did the early church fathers overlook this issue, or did they also strive to keep the hair length of Christians in a godly fashion?

One of the earliest church fathers, Clement of Alexandria, had a lot to say about hair. He wrote in his letter, "The Instructor," that men should not allow their hair to "hang far down from the head gliding into womanish ringlets." He also taught that the hair on a man's head "may not grow so long as to come down and interfere with the eyes."[31] Clement continued, "It is enough for women to protect their locks, and bind up their hair simply along the neck with a plain hair-pin, nourishing chaste locks with simple care to true beauty."[32]

The simplicity of hair care was the central focus of Clement's teaching in this portion of his letter. He did not want women to get caught up with the elaborate hairstyles of that day, which took from six to ten hours to fix. "For meretricious plaiting of the hair," he declared, "and putting it up in tresses, contribute to make them look ugly."[33] He also proceeded to instruct women not to wear wigs. There were no synthetic fibers during those days to make wigs, so many were made from the hair of deceased persons.

"Cutting the hair," Clement advised, "and plucking off it those treacherous braidings; on account of which they do not touch their head, being afraid of disordering their hair. . . . But additions of other people's hair are entirely to be rejected and it is a most sacrilegious thing for spurious hair to shade the head covering the skull with dead locks."[34] They thought that the sins of the dead person remained in the hair, so when a woman wore the wig she would "fall into double sins." He continued, "For on whom does the presbyter lay his hand? Not the woman decked out, but another's hair, and through them another head."[35]

---

31. Clement of Alexandria, "The Instructor," *Ante-Nicene Fathers*, Alexander Roberts and James Donaldson (eds. and trans.), vol. 2 (Grand Rapids: Eerdmans, rpt. 1971), 286.
32. Ibid.
33. Ibid.
34. Ibid.
35. Ibid.

The women of Clement's time wore wigs for aesthetic or ornamental reasons. The women wanted to look more attractive. There was no mention of women wearing wigs because they lost their hair due to medical treatments or serious illness. In our modern day, some ladies deem it necessary to wear wigs until their hair grows out long enough to fix nicely.

The hair length struggle continued and was reflected in the letters of other Nicene fathers. Some church fathers admonished their hearers to use the guidelines of nature. Tertullian (AD 160?-230?), describing the teaching of nature, wrote in his letter, "The Chaplet," "We first of all indeed know God Himself by the teaching of Nature, calling Him God of gods, taking for granted that is He good, and invoking Him as Judge."[36]

He continued:

> It is as much against nature to long after a flower with the head, as it is to crave food with the ear, or sound with nostril. . . . Is it a question with you whether for the enjoyment of His creatures, Nature should be our guide, that we may not be carried away in the direction in which the rival of God has corrupted . . . the apostle says that it [creation] too unwillingly became subject to vanity, completely bereft of its original character, first by vain, then by base, unrighteous, and ungodly uses? . . . But everything which is against nature deserves to be branded as monstrous among all men; but with us it is to be condemned also as sacrilege against God, the Lord and Creator of nature. [37]

Tertullian affirmed that nature itself will teach us. All we need to do is just adhere to it, and that which is against nature should be abhorred, he counseled.

St. Ambrose (AD 340?-397), Bishop of Milan, told us that what is

---

36. Tertullian, "The Chaplet," *Ante-Nicene Fathers*, Roberts and Donaldson (eds. and trans.), vol. 3 (Grand Rapids: Eerdmans, rpt. 1971), 96.
37. Ibid.

according to nature is virtuous, and what is otherwise must be looked on as shameful. He declared:

> It is seemly to live in accordance with nature, and to pass our time in accordance with it, and that whatever is contrary to nature is shameful . . . 'if a man have long hair, it is a shame' . . . for it is contrary to nature . . . but 'if a woman has long hair, it is a glory unto her.' It is according to nature, since her hair is given her for a veil, for it is a natural veil. Thus, nature arranges for us both character and appearance, and we ought to observe her directions. Would that we could guard her innocence, and not change what we have received by our wickedness![38]

Perhaps the most famous of all letters written during the Nicene and Post-Nicene fathers' era was that of St. Jerome, who lived circa AD 340-420. His letter to Eustochium contains a vivid picture of the Roman society as it was then. He was wrestling with the problems of luxury, profligacy, and hypocrisy that were prevalent among both men and women in the church. He wrote:

> And when you come into a room full of brothers and sisters, do not sit in too low a place or plead that you are unworthy of a footstool. Do not deliberately lower your voice as though worn out with fasting; nor, leaning on the shoulder of another, to mimic the tottering gait of one who is faint. Some women, it is true, disfigure their faces, that they may appear unto men to fast. As soon as they catch sight of any one they groan, they look down; they cover up their faces, all but one eye, which they keep free to see with. Their dress is sombre, their girdles are of sackcloth, their hands and feet are dirty; only their stomachs—which cannot be seen are hot with

---

38. St. Ambrose, "Duties of the Clergy," *The Nicene and Post-Nicene Fathers*, 2nd series, Philip Schaff and Henry Wace (eds. and trans.), vol. 10 (Grand Rapids: Eerdmans, 1954), 37.

> food. Of these the Psalm is sung daily: 'The Lord will scatter the bones of them that please themselves.' Others change their garb and assume the mien of men, being ashamed of being what they were born to be—women. They cut off their hair and are not ashamed to look like eunuchs.[39]

St. Jerome struggled with the Roman converts during his day. He stated that some of the women were shamelessly cutting their hair so short that they looked like "eunuchs." Without the sting of conscience, women defied the laws of God even when in those days it was still a disgrace for a woman to look like a man.

"What is seemly should always shine forth in our lives," St. Ambrose once said.[40] It is "seemly" or right for a woman to look feminine with her long, uncut hair, but the man should look masculine with his short, cut hair. Elide writes, "We may find that long hair is considered appropriate to the female sex because it appears soft and rounded, while close-cropped hair is associated with males because it allows the shape of the skull to appear, giving an appropriately hard and angular appearance."[41] The hair length principle is taught not only in God's Word but also as one of nature's indispensable lessons.

The Middle Ages

The struggle to keep the hair worn in a godly fashion continued through the Middle Ages. In the seventh century, for example, there was a fierce difference of opinion between the See of Rome and the Catholic church of England, Scotland, and Ireland. The pope won the argument and insisted that the use of the razor for men was "indispensable to salvation."[42]

The priests of France persisted to admonish its male parishioners

---

39. St. Jerome, "Letter to Eustochium," *The Nicene and Post-Nicene Fathers*, 2nd series, Schaff and Wace (eds. and trans.), vol. 12 (Grand Rapids: Eerdmans, 1954), 34.

40. St. Ambrose, 38.

41. Elide, 154.

42. Cooper, 102.

to keep their hair short. William the Conqueror led his Normans into the Battle of Hastings, and most of his men were clean shaven with their hair clipped short to their ears. When William I, King of England, defeated Harold at the Battle of Hastings in 1066, he forced his British subjects to shave and cut their hair in accordance with the teachings of the church. Many complied, but those who resisted were threatened with excommunication.

However, Bishop Wulstan of Worcester took matters into his own hands by carrying with him a sharp knife. Whenever a long-haired penitent male knelt to receive his blessing, the bishop would pull out his knife, lop off a lock of the "criminal and beastly" hair, and throw it in the man's face.[43]

In 1096 the archbishop of Rouen proclaimed anyone wearing long hair or a beard should be excluded from the church, both before and after death. Instead King Henry I, in 1102, gave up shaving altogether and grew his hair long, supposedly the reason being there was a shortage of soap. But Bishop Serlo of Seez in Normandy denounced King Henry I and his men for this action. His plea was so moving that he persuaded the king "to give up his locks" and clipped off the king's hair and beard, along with those of his nobles. When there was no more hair to trim, the court stomped their feet on the shorn locks "to crush out the evil."[44]

Not much is known about hair from the twelfth century to the sixteenth except for some writings by Albertus Magnus (1193-1280), Guy de Chauliac (1300-1370), Henri de Mondeville (1260-1320), and Arnold of Villanova (1235-1312), in which they discussed the problems of personal adornment.[45]

Perhaps many men during these 433 years wore their hair long. It is known that King Francis I of France in 1521 cut his hair short, but it was not because of religious convictions. The king was a practical joker; one night he wanted to have a snowball fight with some of his knights. They decided to bombard the home of a Count Montgomery in a mock attack. However, in the frivolity someone threw a flaming torch to the

43. Severn, 32.
44. Severn, 33, and Cooper, 102.
45. Goodman, 267.

king's head, which burned him badly. He had to be shaven clean in order to let the wounds heal. His courtiers showed their sympathy by also shaving their heads. Soon it became a fashion statement rather than a conviction.[46]

After four hundred years of men possibly wearing their hair long past their shoulders, King Henry VIII "commanded all about his Court to poll their heads," according to *Stow's Annals of 1535*. To be a good example of the new edict, the king polled his own head. It was said that Henry VIII really admired the new fashion of King Francis I, so he too joined the royal ranks of the shorn.[47]

In a few decades, noblemen were back to wearing long hair. But the growing Puritan sect in England stood up for the biblical principle of hair. They believed it was not only a royal decadence but a sin against God. William Prynne was one of the most outspoken Puritan pamphleteers of his time. In 1628 he published a sixty-three-page denunciation of long hair on men, *The Unloveliness of Lovelocks.*[48] Later, he wrote against the evils of the theater, Histrio-Mastix (1633), that resulted in his imprisonment and the amputation of his ears. He was later imprisoned for politically agitative writings and was branded on both cheeks.[49]

In 1653, Thomas Hall, pastor of Kingsnorton, attacked long hair on men as well, by writing *Comarum, The Loathsomnesse of Long Hair*. His piece was twice as long as Prynne's dissertation.

Through the seventeenth and eighteenth centuries, noblemen started the ancient fashion of wearing wigs that flowed down their backs. The church leaders, all the while, contended bitterly against it. They fought, denounced, and proclaimed God's Word against this evil.

Governor John Endecott, missionary John Elliot, and judge Samuel Sewell were a few men who stood up against long-haired men and Periwig makers.[50] Soon, however, the men forgot about their own feuding with each other's long hair, wigs, and beards to try to stop the outlandish hairdos of the women.

---

46. Severn, 34.
47. Ibid.
48. Ibid., 40.
49. "William Prynne," *American Heritage Dictionary*, CD-ROM.
50. Severn, 50-53.

The Decameron

The Ladies in the Middle Ages

For centuries the ladies had modestly hidden their hair from male view, until 1547 when Italian, French, and English women began to puff their hair out with pads and wires.

The Queen of England and Ireland, Elizabeth I, reigned and succeeded the Catholic Mary I (1533-1603). She reestablished Protestantism in England.[51] Many believed that she was bald, but in reality she shaved her thinning sandy hair. She ignored the dictum of I Corinthians 11 to keep her hair long and covered her shorn locks with wigs that were dyed red. The queen had more than eighty wigs in different styles.

Her rival, Mary I, Queen of Scots (1587), trying to outdo Elizabeth I, had as many wigs if not more. In prison, Queen Mary I changed her auburn wigs every day. At her death, it is said she wore her favorite wig to the executioner's block.[52]

For a while women wore their hair quite simple, . . . but perhaps they were unwittingly getting ready to set a hair revolution in motion. The most outrageous hairstyles were yet to come in the late seventeenth century and would continue into the eighteenth century.

Madame de Pompadour, mistress of France's Louis XV, started the new upward trend in mid-century by arranging her hair "in a

51. "Mary I, Queen of Scots," *American Heritage Dictionary*.
52. Severn, 38.

hundred entrancing ways . . . until the court nearly went mad attempting to imitate her inimitable coiffures."[53]

With one fell swoop, the women's hairstyles progressed upward until they "rivaled the Alps." The pompadour began by being padded, puffed, stuffed, and swept up over wire frames. They added false hair to make it tower higher still, sometimes reaching nearly three feet. Artists mocked, writers ridiculed, and furious males wrote angry letters to the newspapers, but the women seemed to ignore the threats to gloat in their ascending hairstyles.

The hair creations were described as "monstrous." Bushels of cotton wool, shreds of rope, horsehair, bran or straw were used for stuffing, mounded upon felt pads or cap wigs, with the natural hair brought up over the wire frames and masses of false hair added. The whole thing was cemented with a paste that hardened, and the outer shell was greased and floured with powder, decorated with gauze, tulle, pearls, and jewels. Creating this headdress required a full day's time.[54]

Once the structure was constructed, it was left on the lady's head for two to nine weeks. Many women slept with their necks on wooden supports to preserve their artificial "heads." This also caused the rebuilding of some homes, to raise ceilings and widen doorways. Even so, women sometimes had to enter rooms on their knees and kneel on the floors, sedan chairs, and carriages, or else hang their head out the window of the carriage. In the case of Marie Antoinette, the wife of Louis XVI, upon departing for the ball in 1776, her headdress was so high that she could not get into her carriage; therefore, her headdress was taken off.[55] It may have been because of the ten exorbitant ostrich feathers that stood so high.

It must have been quite a sight to behold. Some of the critic's objections were that the hairdo itself began to carry a foul odor. One letter writer agreed that "attracted by my eyes to approach as near as I could to these beautiful creatures, I have soon been repelled by my nose and been obliged to retire at a respectful distance."[56] When it was time to take the hair down, they were surprised at what crawled out. One report

53. Ibid., 67.
54. Ibid., 68.
55. Cooper, 95.
56. Severn, 68.

explained the discovery of a nest of mice, and another said that when a lady's hair was opened up, swarms of "animalculas" were running around.

"No period produced such preposterous and grotesque extravaganzas of hair as the 18th century."[57] The most absurd example of extremism is that of Madame de Lauzun. She wore an enormously high headdress of hair and artificial hair. On top of the structure were modeled ducks swimming in a stormy sea, scenes of hunting and shooting, a mill with a miller's wife flirting with a priest, and the miller leading a donkey by its halter.

The trouble with these kinds of exuberant hairstyles was that after the novelty wore off, they were soon commonplace. There was always someone endeavoring to supersede the latest creation with an even more elaborate hairdo.

As the contention between the men was distracted by the extravagance of the women's hairdos, they became very outspoken against this inordinate behavior of the women. Their argument was not so much for hygienic reasons as much as they said it was "immoral." Philip Stubbes, in *The Anatomie of Abuses*, attacked the Elizabethan women's fashion:

> So whereas their haire was given them as a signe of subjection, and therefore they were commanded to cherish the same, now have they made it an ornament of pride, and destruction to themselves for ever, excepte they repent.[58]

57. Cooper, 95.
58. Severn, 37-38.

The hairstyles began to descend during the Victorian Era. There were those, mostly the rich, who still bought false locks to wear in their chignon hairstyles. Most of the hair was imported from London, which later became a very lucrative business.

Some hairdos of the later Victorian Era look very much like today's Pentecostal holiness ladies' hairstyles.

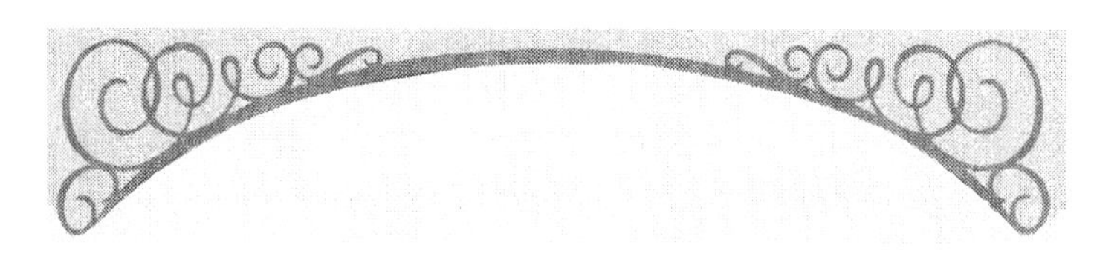

5 – The Decline of Religious America

Josh McDowell, traveling speaker, instructor, and author, once said, "History shows that when a generation fails to know 'why' they believe what they believe, their convictions are in danger of being undermined." We cannot fail to tell our generation "why" consecrated women of God do not cut their hair. However, the spiritual laws of God are seldom explained in two or three blanket statements as are the carnal, physical laws of man.

To get a clearer understanding of the "whys," we will first take a look back at "how" hair cutting came about in our history. We will examine some thought-provoking questions as well: Was there a time when long hair on ladies was the everyday norm? When did ladies start cutting their hair? Who started the short hair trend? And what effects did this have on our nation as a whole?

A Look Back

"One hundred years ago," says Segraves, "to insist that a woman's hair was her glory would not have been thought strange anywhere in Christendom, regardless of a person's denominational affiliation or lack of it."[1] Women everywhere, churchgoers or not, kept their hair long and uncut. In several books on the nation's history, one can read that hair on a lady's head was regarded as her "crowning glory."

Just by looking in any encyclopedia under "hair," we can easily trace the trend of hair cutting to the turn of the twentieth century. As we glance through a century of our nation's history, we readily observe the degenerating spiral of godliness. From decade to decade until this day and age, our nation's morals have come to be virtually extinct.

According to Time-Life Books in their prelude volume, *This*

1. Segraves, 50.

Fabulous Century 1870-1900, "In a still religious America, she [the woman] heeded the New Testament dictum that 'if a woman have long hair, it is a glory to her'; she never cut it, but in this period of primness, she also never let it fall unfettered to her waist.[2] Instead, she piled it on her head in the 1870s, arranged it in ringlets in the 1880s, and arrayed it to frame her face in the 1890s."

Victorian women

The death of Queen Victoria in 1901 brought an end to the noble-minded culture. Her sense of duty and strict moral code had a great influence on nineteenth-century Great Britain as well as on America. Preaching at a church one day on "Why we must have revival," Rev. Lee Stoneking asserted, "Queen Victoria was the greatest reigning monarch in all of England's history. She was a deeply religious woman who loved Jesus Christ very much. She believed in Jesus so much that she wanted Him to return during her earthly reign so that she could take her crown off and lay it at His feet. There is a painting in the National Gallery showing the queen and many other monarchs of her day laying their crowns at the feet of Jesus."[3] However, all of Queen Victoria's godly influence was soon to change after her death.

Some felt that since the queen was dead they could confront the high standards that were set in motion during her sixty-four-year reign. After all, her successor, Edward VII, had acquired a reputation as a playboy. Although his reign was a short nine years, society still challenged the moral codes. Not only did changes take place technolog-

---

2. Hedley Donovan (ed.), *This Fabulous Century 1870-1900*, prelude (New York: Time-Life Books, 1970), 190.

3. Lee Stoneking, "Why we must have revival," 14 November, 1985, tape.

ically, but also there were changes in this country's mores.

Just prior to the turn of the century, our land was known as the "nation on the move." An article that ran in the *New York Herald*, January 1, 1876, records, "The last hundred years have been the most fruitful and the most glorious period of equal length in the history of the human race. . . . We are entering a year which will be ever memorable in our annals."[4]

The nation was enjoying the exhilarating conditions of life, especially the sentiments of the celebration in 1876, the hundredth anniversary of the nation's founding. Just six years prior, in 1869, the completion of the railroad gave the nation another satisfied feeling of accomplishment. In many ways it brought healing to the war-torn country. Soon many people, goods, and ideas began to travel from coast to coast. A treacherous journey of one month by wagon or shipboard became a pleasure trip of seven days by train.

Our nation was living under the covering of grace that God so generously placed upon it. People ran the risk of losing their grip on spiritual pursuits with all their technical growth and achievements. The Bible says in Titus 2:11-13, ***The grace of God that bringeth salvation hath appeared to all men, teaching us that, denying ungodliness and worldly lusts, we should live soberly, righteously, and godly, in this present world; looking for that blessed hope, and the glorious appearing of the great God and our Saviour Jesus Christ.***

The eyes of America began to wander off the soon coming of the Lord. Their resistance to ungodliness and worldly lusts began to waver during the next few decades.

The First Few Decades

By the time of the twentieth century, most Americans felt optimistic and self-confident to such an extreme that they did not merely hope for the best; they fully expected it. Thus, this age was known as the "Cocksure Era." The first decade won several additional titles—the Age of Optimism, the Age of Confidence, and the Age of Innocence. "The

4. Donovan, 25.

will to grow was everywhere written large, and to grow at no matter what or whose expense," says Henry James, in the book, *This Fabulous Century 1900-1910.*[5]

Technology was at its highest yet. The telephone, typewriter, and self-binding harvester were all in full swing. The Sears Roebuck catalog became the wish book of every woman. Many ladies got the new, innovative items to make their housekeeping chores less strenuous.

By 1900, eight thousand citizens owned the newly invented automobile. In no time at all, most of America became involved with the present-day auto craze, and by 1906, the auto fad became a fancy. In 1908 Henry Ford produced his first Model T, and by 1909 ten thousand people already owned their new set of wheels. Hence, Americans were on their way of forging the mobile culture. Historian Ralph Andrist stated in *American Century: One Hundred Years of Changing Life Styles in America*, "The automobile was to be the principal agent of destruction of this easygoing way of life."[6]

This was the pivotal point, where the decline of spirituality in America started. Slowly our country began to leave her love for God to love the things of this world. Her sensitivity to His Word was soon thwarted. The strong morals and manners America once knew drove away with the car. Instead of families being in church on Sunday to hear the Word of God, many were tempted to get on the roads to head for the theater. The Book of James 4:4 cautions, ***Know ye not that the friendship of the world is enmity with God? whosoever therefore will be a friend of the world is the enemy of God***.

By the second decade, many people were becoming restless. "America is in a period of clamor, of bewilderment, of an almost tremulous unrest. We are hastily reviewing all our social conceptions. We are profoundly disenchanted," said Walter Weyl in "The New Democracy," 1912.[7]

Even though economic growth had tripled, with many enjoying the

---

5. Maitland A. Edley (ed.), *This Fabulous Century 1900-1910*, vol. 1 (New York: Time-Life Books, 1969), 29.

6. Ralph Andrist, *American Century: One Hundred Years of Changing Life Styles in America* (New York: American Heritage Press, 1972), 146.

7. Edley, "The New Democracy," vol. 2, 23.

wealth of the "good life," the nation's atmosphere was full of discontent and intense ferment. Rev. James K. Thompson in Muskogee, Oklahoma, on June 28, 1914, cried out in his sermon, "Whither Are We Drifting?" about the various changes.[8] It was the theme used by many preachers, yet no one seemed to know the answer.

Those who stood for biblical principles could sense in many people the falling away from spiritual truths. I can hear the cry of the apostle Paul's warning in Colossians 2:8: ***Beware lest any man spoil you through philosophy and vain deceit, after the tradition of men, after the rudiments of the world, and not after Christ.***

Numerous changes were taking place all over our nation and at a torrential speed! Labor workers ignited no less than 2,094 strikes and lockouts. Many other militant demonstrators were campaigning for causes that seemed radical for that day; to name a few: the six-day workweek, women's suffrage, birth control, advancement for colored people, progressive education, and prohibition. Most alarming of all, a million socialists were demanding the overthrow of capitalism.[9] All citizens were crying out for change.

Although World War I had broken out during this time in Europe 1914, America didn't get involved until the declaration of war by President Woodrow Wilson against Germany on April 2, 1917. This brought about the biggest changes in the lives of American women. The war presented women with fresh opportunities to employ their talents and abilities. In reality, however, they were left with no choice but to help support their "doughboys." The women had to leave their homes to work while the men went to a foreign land to fight in the war.

Male-dominated America was confronted suddenly with the spectacle of women auto mechanics, telegraph messengers, elevator operators, bomb assemblers, and streetcar conductors. Many women toiled in factories, carried ice, plowed fields, and became traffic cops. Some eleven thousand female yeomen enlisted in the navy for shore duty, and 269 ladies were clerks and stenographers in the Marine Corps.[10]

---

8. Ibid.
9. Ibid.
10. Ibid., 219.

After the War

By the time the war had ended on November 11, 1918, the women of America had proven to be competent workers. Yet when all the celebrations were over and the dust was settled, the guys expected the women to run along home and stay put! Many had forgotten that it was the total commitment by women and children during the war that had kept the number of casualties from reaching an exorbitant amount, instead keeping the rate under 13 percent.[11]

It wasn't easy to return to the pre-war way of life. Nothing could ever be the same after being stained by a world war. Women felt the same sense of pride as the men for taking part in the victory over the enemy. Soon, however, America went back to her internal fussing and confusion. Demonstrators marched the streets, vying for change.

In the midst of all this turmoil, the ladies were pressing for their own validation. Professors Divine, Breen, Fredrickson, and Williams remind us that just a hundred years prior Abigail Adams had encouraged her husband, John, as he set off for the opening of the Continental Congress, "I desire you would Remember the Ladies, and be more generous and favorable to them than our ancestors. Do not put such unlimited power in the hands of the Husbands."[12]

Up to this time in the 1770s, domestic violence was an everyday occurrence for some. Women were treated as the mere property of their husbands; that often vindicated severe beatings. Until 1773, women could not successfully obtain their freedom from such tyranny by suing for divorce. Mrs. Adams stated if women were denied rights, a rebellion would foment. She was right, for 125 years later, some fifteen thousand women rallied on the streets on their cities. And on June 4, 1919, they were granted the right to vote. Perhaps, if the authors of the Declaration of Independence heeded this First Lady's warning, the necessary evil of

11. Thomas B. Allen (ed.), *We Americans: A Volume in the Story of Man Library* (Washington, DC: National Geographic Society, 1975), 383.

12. Robert A. Divine, T. H. Breen, George M. Fredrickson, and R. Hall Williams, *America Past and Present* (Glenview: Scott, Foresman and Company, 1984), 155.

feminism might never have taken root.[13]

Some people were not happy with the Congress passing the nineteenth amendment to the Constitution, while others were thrilled, like the Democratic candidate for President, James Cox. He jumped at the prospect of receiving an extra 26 million votes from the women.[14]

"We take this voting privilege for granted," says Maggie Pexton Murray in her book, *Changing Styles in Fashion: Who, What, Why*, "but in our grandmother's time, women did not vote. They were not allowed to. This struggle for freedom, the right to work, the right to leave home, the right to vote, made its mark on the fashion."[15] Not only fashion was affected but also upcoming trends and hairstyles.

1920s, Decade of Decadence

By the time the 1920s rolled around, society was about to make a quantum leap into the pit of rebellion. The revolt was against God and His holy ordinances. A spirit of frivolity seized our country. Materialism flourished like a wild branch, as the country was spending its wages on everything from automobiles to washing machines.

With all the new technology, women were becoming more and more visible as their household chores were becoming easier and easier. They could get things done quicker so that they had more time to do other activities.

Just what was going on to influence the surge of defiance? Many believe that the fashion of women bobbing their hair [cutting it short] was caused directly by the "feminist movement" and single out the "demanding women pushing for equality." But as you read further, you'll find there was more to it even before the feminists copped its identity.

The '20s became the era known as the "First Youth Rebellion." It rained on the country like a deluge. The youth were bursting with energy, wanting freedom from the older generation's authority.

---

13. Mary Cable, *American Manners and Morals* (New York: American Heritage Publishing, 1969), 264.
14. Edley, 48.
15. Maggie Pexton Murray, *Changing Styles in Fashion: Who, What, Why* (New York: Fairchild Publications, 1989), 103.

Morals, too, were undergoing a revolution. Sigmund Freud's sex theories became household chatter. His ungodly psychology was replacing biblical principles. More and more boys were owning automobiles—and parking them on dark roads to "neck" with their dates. Thus, the call for gaiety and fun was louder than the cry for decency.

Jazz was the thriving music. Musicians came out with all kinds of new dance moves. The newfound dance crazes—like the Charleston, Turkey Trot, and Bunny Hug—caught hold of many, even the "respectable citizens." The dances brought men and women together, cheek to cheek, thigh to thigh. Most women dancers were known as "flappers."

Gambling, drinking, and smoking were at their all-time highest. The Prohibition in 1920 could not stop the flood of whiskey sippers and bathtub gin drinkers. Speakeasies were springing up in all the big cities. Illegal drugs were slowly becoming available on the streets.

The silent movies became America's favorite pastime. Then the new fad became "the talking picture shows." Young people would copy many outrageous fashions that Hollywood would spew out.

The rebirth of hate groups such as the Ku Klux Klan demonstrated its strength as forty thousand men marched before the nation's capitol. Racism's tide was coming in fast.

All these outside influences made the age a prime time for the women to want to change their stereotypical image. However, the right to vote and the new sense of freedom went straight to the women's heads. They had a mistaken enthusiasm. They wanted to do manly things; that is, things that were thought to be appropriate for men only.

Women proved they could do jobs and take responsibility during and after the war, so they pushed to be equally valued with men. In reality, they wanted freedom to do the things men were known to enjoy doing freely . . . however sinful they were. Smoking, drinking, gambling, or taking drugs by a man or woman—it's still sin in God's eyes.

The women of the 1920s went too far in wanting their validation. They carried their rebellion to extremes. They actually were trying to make "men" out of themselves. It's okay to want a job, want validation, or take part in society, but when you have to transgress God's laws to get there, you enter dangerous territory with violation to Scripture. Jesus reminds us of this principle in Mark 8:36, ***For what shall it profit a man, if he shall gain the whole world, and lose his own soul?***

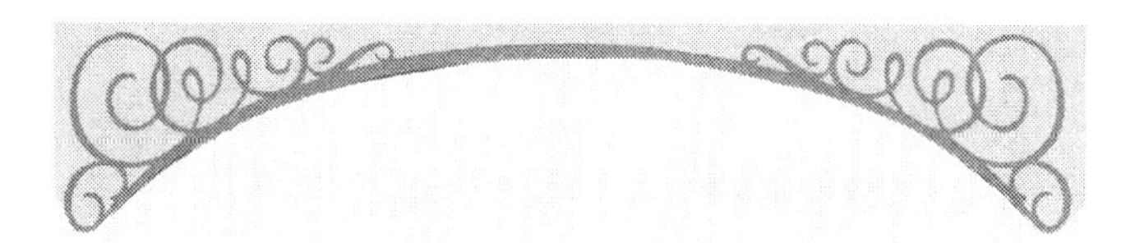

6 – Bobbed Hair Makes History

The wedge of rebellion was driven by immorality to split the godly foundations established for many generations. Perhaps the generation before failed to tell its youth "why" they believed what they believed. They saw the woman's long hair as nothing more than a tradition of their culture, a teaching of a "church," but not a pure biblical truth to live by. Therefore, with no solid foundation on God's Word, the generation of the '20s tumbled spiritually to the ground. If any American women knew the laws of God, they willfully disregarded them to follow the fashion of trend-setter, Irene Castle.

The Bobbed Hair Trend

Irene Foote was born in New Rochelle, New York, April 7, 1893. At the age of seven, she was sent to St. Mary's Episcopal Convent, Peekskill, New York, and later attended National Park Seminary near Washington, DC. Despite her father's reservations, she married her dance partner, Vernon Castle, in 1911.

They sailed to France in 1912, where a chance engagement at the Café de Paris led them to fame. Between national tours in America, the Castles opened several dance schools and nightclubs and wrote a ballroom dancing textbook, *Modern Dancing*, published in 1914.[1]

She began to wear ankle-length dancing skirts, which was unheard of during floor-length fashion. "Irene Castle was the most famous ballroom dancer of her time," says Lois Decker O'Neill in her book, *The Women's Book of World Records and Achievements.*[2] At the age of

---

1. "Irene Castle," *Grolier Multimedia Encyclopedia*, CD-ROM.

2. Lois Decker O'Neill (ed.), "Most Influential Fashion Figure of the Decade 1910-1920" and "First American-Born Hat Designer," *The Women's Book of World Records and Achievements* (Garden City: Anchor Press/Doubleday, 1979), 238.

twenty-two, in 1915 Castle felt she needed to bob her hair for the convenience and freedom it lent her in dancing.

According to Richard Corson in his book, *Fashion in Hair: The First Five Thousand Years*, Irene Castle walked into the little room where hairstylist Signor Pierro Raspanti "presided over manicure tables and hairdressing chairs in a New York department store. She demanded a bob . . . saying, 'Ten years from now, mark my word, half of the women will wear their hair short.' . . . A vogue was started that has far exceeded the prophecy of its originator."[3]

She threw away the hairpins to introduce the headband to hold her "Castle frocks" in place. Gradually, her new "Eton Crop" hairstyle that originated in Paris was becoming popular in America, but it didn't really spark aflame until 1923, when Lilly Dache sold new hat shapes in her shop to go with the bobbed hairdos.[4]

It was just a short span of three years after Irene Castle cut her hair that her honeymoon-marriage came to an abrupt end in an airplane crash. The sudden death of her husband in 1918 left Irene devastated. Her second marriage lasted only four years to end in divorce, and in 1933 her performing career was winding to an end. Her third marriage was no better than the previous one, causing her to endure several years of conflict. In 1937 she eventually ended up living in an separate residence from her spouse and operating her own animal shelter.[5]

---

3. Richard Corson, *Fashion in Hair: The First Five Thousand Years* (New York: Hastings House, 1965), 610-611.

4. O'Neill, 238.

5. Barbara Sicherman and Carol Hurd Green (eds.), "Irene Castle," *Noble American Women: The Modern Period 1607-1950* (Massachusetts: Belknap Press, 1980), 142-143.

Bobbed Hair Becomes National News

During the '20s no national issue aroused its citizens like that of the bobbed hair. One librarian at San Jose State University who helped me to research the archives commented that the bobbed hair issue in the '20s must have been like the O. J. Simpson case. "There hasn't been a newspaper printed for the past two years . . . that hasn't carried some sort of little story . . . about women's hair. . . . It used to be a woman's crowning glory, but now it's just hair," said Marian Spitzer in her article, "The Erstwhile Crowning Glory," printed in *The Saturday Evening Post*, June 27, 1925.[6]

Some of the articles I managed to find that were written in response to the new bobbed hair trend are: "Does Your Hair Reveal Your Character?" published by *Popular Mechanics*, June 1926; "HAIR—Woman's Glory and Man's Despair" by *Hygeia* (health magazine), July 1927, "Some Bald Facts," *Hygeia*, October 1927; "Hair," *Scientific American*, November 1927; "Surprising New Facts about Hair," *Science and Discovery*, April 1925.

Several more articles were written, but I couldn't obtain them. Some of the titles sounded interesting to me: "Hair, The Growing Question," *Sunset*, April 1928; "What Price Your Crowning Glory?" *Sunset*, June 1925; "Economic Effects of Hair-bobbing," *Literary Digest*, September 1926; "If You Are Letting It Grow," *Pictorial Review*, April 1928; "Superfluous Hair," *Good Housekeeping*, March 1925; "Troubles with Bobbed Hair," *Good Housekeeping*, October 1927; "Your Personality and the Bob," *Delineator*, November 1927.

Many articles were written in defense of the bobbed hairdo, such

6. Marian Spitzer, "The Erstwhile Crowning Glory," *The Saturday Evening Post*, 27 June, 1925.

as "Please May I Bob My Hair?" It was written by Mary Pickford and published in *Liberty Magazine*, April 1927. Throughout her article, she wrote as if she were seeking approval to bob her hair. Pickford wrestled with the question to bob or not to bob.

In one sentence she said that a woman looks smarter with a bob; then in another sentence she said that shaved necks are "dreadful and they take away all charm and femininity from the most attractive woman." She stated that when she mentions her desire to bob her hair, she gets a "deluge of criticism, ranging all the way from a mild reproof to a violent denunciation" from her family, her maid, and her fans. "If I do that all would be distressed and shocked."[7]

She continued to express in all the arguments for and against hair bobbing that she could not understand what the fuss was about. "Except for sentiment and tradition, I can not think of a single argument in favor of long hair. Many are becoming aroused over the sacrilege of destroying old idols, and deploring the loss of woman's 'crowning glory.' "[8]

Pickford stated that bobbed hair is "for comfort and convenience and all arguments favor short hair." With an attempt to restore charm and admiration for short bobbed hair, Pickford wrote, "I haven't yet met the woman who has enjoyed the freedom and comfort of short hair and wants to return to hairpins and all the annoyances of long hair."[9] Nothing was mentioned in her article about what the Bible says about a woman's hair. Most women who cut their hair nowadays do not really know what I Corinthians 11:6, 14-15 teaches. Like Pickford, the women in the twenty-first century say it's for convenience and comfort.

Fashion was not the case in Asian countries during the '20s, but

---

7. Mary Pickford, "Please May I Bob My Hair?" *Liberty Magazine*, April 1927, *The Liberty Years 1924-1950: An Anthology*, Allen Churchill (ed.) (New Jersey: Prentice-Hall, 1969), 10-12.

8. Ibid.

9. Ibid.

hair cutting was a money-making scheme. The editorial section of *Scientific American Digest* of 1927 reported that "human hair imports from China have been increasing steadily since the beginning of the year. In January shipments were 21,334 pounds. By April, they had more than doubled: 59,438 pounds valued at 20,110 dollars."[10] The article did not state what they planned to do with the hair, but my guess is that they would make wigs.

According to Kirstin Olsen, in *Chronology of Women's History*, "The Korean government started hiring their women for the first time in the Modern Era. Several young women who took the jobs at the royal mint decided to cut off their long hair as a sign of independence."[11]

Spitzer, in the article I mentioned earlier, argued against women's short hair. "There is nothing that looks quite so unkempt and ragged as bobbed hair. It must be trimmed constantly." She offered a couple of reasons why women continued to cut their hair in the '20s, "There are a great many women who will never let their hair grow again; some because they don't want to and others because they somehow cannot get past that trying period when it is neither long nor short, and who, with firmest of intentions to let it grow, always snip it off again when it gets down to about the shoulders."[12]

Spitzer noticed that many of the women later regretted cutting it. "There is among these women a definitely felt want that has begun to manifest itself. The best reason ever given by a woman for not bobbing her hair is because if your hair is short you can't take it down, women like to take their hair down." She explained that part of a woman's femininity is playing with her long hair. "There is probably not a woman in the world who has not at some time sat enthralled before her mirror, experimenting with her hair, trying new ways to fix it."[13]

With some ladies it wasn't pure feminist rebellion that caused them to cut their hair but a plain, old-fashioned desire for a new hairdo. Thus, some jumped at the chance of getting a new "do." "One of the reasons

---

10. *Scientific American Digest*, April 1927.

11. Kirstin Olsen, *Chronology of Women's History* (Westport: Greenwood, 1994), 169.

12. Spitzer.

13. Ibid.

why many women bobbed their hair in the first place was curiosity. But after the novelty wears off there is not much you can do with it."[14] Again, in this article there was no mention of "what saith the Word of God." This generation simply didn't have knowledge of the scriptural principle found in I Corinthians 11:14, 15 like the past decades had.

In 1925, Julia Hoyt wrote, "It certainly begins to look as if a 'woman's crowning glory' is soon going to be a relic of the past. I can picture that some fifty or a hundred years from now, paintings and photographs of women with long flowing hair or with complicated and magnificent coiffeurs, will be exhibited as amusing and interesting curiosities."[15]

In a 1927 *Ladies' Home Journal*, Ann Harding stated in her article, "Your Crowning Glory," "The most radical change in the costume of women in our times has been the change in hair styles. . . . Hair really is the crowning glory of a woman. It lights up her person, it frames her face, it makes a halo around her. No matter how she mangles it, or mistreats it, no matter if she cuts most of it off, her hair still remains the most telling item of her appearance. . . . At least with long hair you have variety, and variety is difficult to achieve with bobbed hair. And now short hair is considered chic. It is also the symbol of the freedom of women. But bobbing the hair won't make you free. It isn't so simple as that."[16]

Ladies' Disgrace, Barber's Delight

In January 1923, the *Barbers' Journal* issued their latest report on the bobbed hairdo. The cutting of women's hair was, they said, "shearing short all the beautiful golden, brown, and black tresses. Womenfolk young and up to fascinating, fatal forty are shedding their respected glory of great pitiful waving locks and spiralled curls in dainty beauty shop baskets and on the barber's shining linoleum."[17]

---

14. Ibid.
15. Corson, 611.
16. Ann Harding, "Your Crowning Glory," *Ladies' Home Journal*, March 1927.
17. Corson, 610.

"The close snip rage is raging worse than ever, and soon, if no indignant act of providence intervenes, masses of soft, lustrous feminine braids so much admired of man since the ape gave him his start will be seen alone on elderly mothers and their surviving mamas."[18]

Signor Raspanti predicted that there would be no long locks to sever, since already 90 percent of the young women and 50 percent of their elders, without age limit, had joined the ranks of the bobbed.[19] Men, however, fumed over the feminine invasion of their barbershops. One barber hung, in a conspicuous place outside his shop, a large sign stating: NO LADIES' HAIR BOBBED IN THIS SHOP. In some cities, long lines of women waited anxiously outside barber shops for their turn for a "boyish bob." Women fought for appointments and cheerfully paid as high as five dollars to get their hair cut by the barbers.[20]

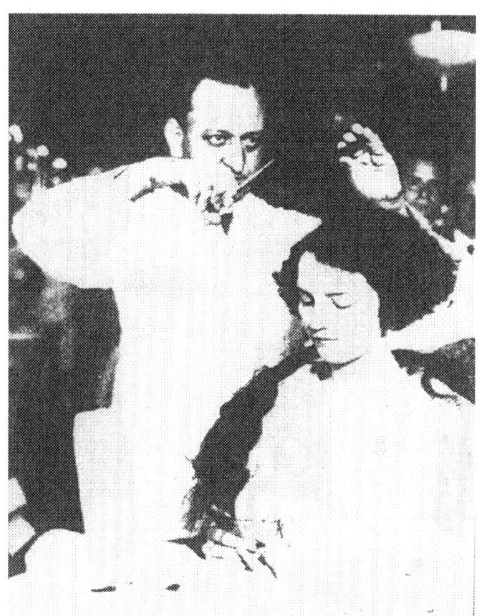

Woman getting her hair bobbed

Mary Brush Williams reported in the *Ladies' Home Journal* in 1925 that she rushed to the hairdresser's only to find to her dismay that the shop was rather crowded with women. After looking at all the women, she felt terribly distressed. She stated in her article that "the girls were sitting on the floor . . . and on one anothers' laps . . ." lingering until it was their turn to get a bob haircut.[21]

The bob hair craze caused all kinds of reactions. Some women were known to faint at the sight of their shorn cascades of crowning glory tumbling to the carpets of the hair salons. Julia Hoyt reported, "I must say that the first snip of

18. Ibid.
19. Ibid., 611.
20. Spitzer.
21. Corson, 612.

the scissors gave me a shock, like a cold bath or taking gas. However, the first moment was the worst."[22]

Raspanti recalled, "There was a time when I had to have smelling salts on my table here, so many women felt faint when they saw their hair was gone. I remember one Frenchwoman who cried and cried. She declared she would not go home; her husband would kill her. I was almost as distressed as she was. I would have given anything to put that hair back where it was. But it was too late. That was the way with many of them then, but it is no longer so. Nowadays they only rejoice in the freedom of bobbed hair."[23]

The bob was, of course, a great boon for barbers and hairdressers. New York alone soon reported heads being clipped at the rate of two thousand a day. It was a case of supply and demand, of course; the world doesn't worry about God's principles in order to make a "buck." Many barbers were virtually getting rich overnight. There was such a demand for bob cuts that barber schools advertised quick courses that would teach the "Boy Bob" to any man's barber.

George E. Darling, defending the bob haircut, said, "It is not a hair style that is preferred by only one class of women—it's the choice of all. . . . Why do . . . people . . . say the bob is going out?" He refuted adamantly the rumors of the dying bobbed hair trend by stating that "people are trying to tear down and destroy one of the greatest professions in this country."[24] He didn't want to see his profitable business go bankrupt. The Bible states in I Timothy 6:10, ***For the love of money is the root of all evil. . . .***

In 1920, there were only five thousand hairdressing shops in the United States, but at the close of 1924 there were twenty-one thousand established shops and several thousand more momentary shops. New shops were opening every day, and they seemed to prosper.[25] In a recent consumer business report, as of 1991 there were 78,588. In 1995 [the time of this book's first printing], the number of beauty shops has possibly risen to over eighty-five thousand.

---

22. Ibid.
23. Ibid., 611.
24. Ibid., 618-619.
25. Spitzer.

Preachers Take a Stand

This was no light thing for the world to swallow. "While fanaticism defies nature, Christianity respects it [nature] and refines it and whatever shocks the common feelings of mankind is not likely to be right."[26] To conservatives, short-haired women were as much "radicals and freaks of society" as long-haired male musicians and artists. Many saw the bobbed hair a symbol of the ills of the "Flaming Youth" era.[27]

As women began to cut their hair, some conservative Christian groups took a stand against it. According to David Bernard in his book, *Practical Holiness: A Second Look*, most of the Holiness groups opposed it, as well as early Pentecostals.[28] Many churches preached adamantly against this wickedness. Most preachers took to pulpits to warn their congregations that a bobbed woman is a disgraced woman.

It was reported in the spring of 1926 that, in a Missouri courtroom, a mother pled for the return of her six children, who had been living with a guardian. Her oldest child, age twelve, was asked by a judge if they wished to return to their mother. She answered "No. We don't believe Mother is a Christian woman. She bobs her hair, and the Bible says in the eleventh chapter of First Corinthians that a woman should not cut her hair. She wears jewelry and bright clothes. A Christian woman shouldn't do these things." The three oldest children were placed in private homes with "Christian influences."[29]

In England, about the same year as the Missouri case, a tract titled "Bobbed Hair: Is It Well-Pleasing to the Lord?" was circulated throughout the country. The author wrote:

> Will our sisters in Christ—the younger ones especially—suffer a few words of exhortation and entreaty? A new fashion has come into the world that knows not God, and many who do know Him are following It. The new fashion

---

26. Robertson and Plummer, 235.
27. Severn, 122.
28. David Bernard, *Practical Holiness: A Second Look* (Hazelwood: Word Aflame Press, 1985), 222.
29. Corson, 614.

is called 'bobbing' the hair! . . . No Christian would willingly grieve the Lord, and assuredly none would knowingly disobey His word. But 'evil is wrought by want of thought as well as want of heart!' . . . The human family, having thrown off God, is a seething mass of restlessness and discontent (Isaiah 7:20-21). No satisfaction can be found. Nothing pleases the mind long, so that those who cater for the world's amusements and fashions have to keep their brains continually on the rack in order to provide something fresh. But why should Christian women fall victims to all this? . . . Has God's word nothing to say concerning these things? Let us turn to 1 Corinthians 11:3-16. In verse 15 we read, ***If a woman has long hair, it is a glory to her: for her hair is given to her for a covering.*** This one passage should suffice for all who wish to please God. . . . In verse 6 we are told that it is ***a shame for a woman to be shorn or shaven.*** The new word 'bobbed' is only another way of saying shorn.

A 'bobbed' woman is a disgraced woman! Surely a very serious consideration for all who fear God! What will the Lord say to our sisters about this when we all stand at His judgment seat? Where would our present-day defaced sisters have been at the scene of the two women who wiped the feet of Jesus? What services could they have rendered the Lord in their unnatural condition? How strangely ill at ease our poor shorn sisters would have been had they been present in the Bethany home that day! . . .

The refusal to utter the word 'obey' in the Marriage Service, the wearing of men's apparel when cycling, the smoking of cigarettes and the 'bobbing' of the hair are all indicative of one thing . . . God's order is everywhere flouted. Divine forbearance tolerates the growing evil for the present, but the hour of Divine intervention in judgment approaches fast.[30]

30. Ibid., 614-615.

This tract tried to warn ladies not to bob their hair. The author expressed the serious offense against God's will. However, the world seemed simply to ignore its warning, and women kept cutting their hair daily. Romans 12:2 states, ***And be not conformed to this world: but be ye transformed by the renewing of your mind, that ye may prove what is that good, and acceptable, and perfect, will of God.***

Men divorced their wives over bobbed hair. One man, John Baer, in Peoria, Illinois, September 27, feared that his temper would get away from him because his wife just bobbed her hair. He called the county jail, begging to be locked up so he could "cool off."[31] The manager of a large department store fired all bobbed-haired employees, and a hospital discharged all bobbed-haired nurses.

The October 1927 edition of *Hygeia*, a health magazine, printed that bobbing would result "in the ultimate baldness of the species."[32] The pull of commercials was strong toward the women; stylists advised that without bobbed hair no woman could hope to be really chic.[33] Some women who chose not to bob their hair simply wore coiled braids, which resembled earphones.

Women were continually faced with the crucial temptation, to bob or not to bob their hair. In an article from 1995, Mary C. Detmers remembers that in 1924, when she was only fourteen years old, she wanted a bobbed hair cut desperately . . . just so she could look like everyone else in her school. But her mother said, "No," and that their hair was their "crowning glory." To cut it would be a sin.[34]

In May 1924, Detmers and her sixteen-year-old sister saw a barber shop open as they were walking home from a picture show one night. They could not resist any longer. Within twenty minutes their hair was lying in heaps on the floor.[35] Though they were punished by having to wear caps to cover their hair for one year, soon their mother succumbed to the pressure and had her own hair bobbed.

---

31. Segraves, 54.
32. *Hygeia*, October 1927.
33. Severn, 122.
34. Mary C. Detmers, "When Bobbed Hair Was 'In,' " *Reminisce Magazine*, Sampler Edition, 1995.
35. Ibid., 28.

Like Detmers, many girls and women chose to ignore the significant biblical principles regarding hair found in I Corinthians 11. In I John 2:15, the Bible tells us and this generation of ladies, ***Love not the world, neither the things that are in the world.*** The *Living Bible* paraphrases this verse in this way, ***Stop loving this evil world and all that it offers you, for when you love these things you show that you do not really love God.***

Bobbed Hair Here to Stay

Perhaps the ladies in the '20s felt that long hair was not pertinent to their newfound lifestyle. The Word of God never changes though the fashion trends do. The hearts of the bobbed-haired women were full of self-will and iniquity. Soon, the hairdo became an international rage. Warsaw, England, East Prussia, and Shanghai were some of the countries that also became outraged at this revolutionary act.[36] The world was soon to reap much calamity from such actions. Was it just because they cut their hair, or was it because this generation turned its back on all that was associated with godliness?

The resistance was strong for women to keep their hair long. Like true royalty, consort Queen Mary was unmoved in 1934 by any of this newfound frenzy of ladies bobbing their hair. An article "Upstairs Downstairs," written by Brian Hoey, which ran in the *Majesty Magazine*, June 1995, stated that a lady who was a housemaid on the principal floor at Buckingham Palace was "told off in the 1930s by Queen Mary for having her hair bobbed, with a sharp comment, 'You are trying to look like a lady.' "[37] This probably meant that the woman was trying to look like a commoner and not like one who associates herself with royalty. Likewise, an order was disseminated by King George for all maid servants in the Buckingham Place, requiring them to keep their hair long, and if they had bobbed their hair, it must be growing back or they would lose their royal jobs.[38]

---

36. Segraves, 54.
37. Brian Hoey, "Upstairs Downstairs," *Majesty Magazine*, June 1995.
38. Segraves, 54.

The liberals, however, rejected any opposition that came their way. They decided to put the feminist identity on the bobbed look. Fifty-year-old opera star, Mary Garden, told readers in her article, "Why I bobbed my hair," that ran in the *Pictorial Review*, April 1927, "Bobbed hair is a state of mind and not merely a new manner of dressing my head. . . . I consider getting rid of our long hair one of the many little shackles that women have cast aside in their passage to freedom. Whatever helps their emancipation, however small it may seem, it is worthwhile. . . . Bobbing hair is one of those things that shows us whether we are abreast of the age in which we find ourselves."[39]

According to this woman, to be "abreast of the age" meant to conform to the world's image. Garden thought that bobbing her hair was a "small thing" that was "worthwhile," but the spiritual consequence for our country was the direst thing in history. During this decade religious America completely backslid into rebellion, iniquity, and wickedness.

There was another outright rebellious article written by Lynn Fontanne, in the *Ladies' Home Journal*, June 1927,

> In sending out this bulletin to American women, I want first of all to ask you to make up your faces. Study makeup. Put it on your faces frankly, boldly—but with artistry. Don't mind what your husbands say. Let them object as loudly as they please. . . . They'll get used to makeup after a while, just as they are getting used to short hair. Not only getting used to it but admiring it and being proud of their wives for being in the know. Short hair not only calls attention to the beautiful shape of one's head, it is chic, which is another way of saying it is a symbol of youth, of the desire to be charming and attractive and of this day and age. . . . Long hair is dangerously on the edge of frumpishness.[40]

At the close of this decade, there was an air of desperation, even among the frivolous. Walter Lippman had said that what most

---

39. Severn, 124.
40. Corson, 616.

distinguishes this generation who had finally matured from the debacle of idealism was not their rebellion against the religion and the moral code of their parents, but their disillusionment with their own rebellion. It left them unchanged and unfulfilled. It is common for young men and women to rebel, but that they should rebel sadly and without faith in their rebellion, that they should distrust the new freedom no less than the old certainties—that is something of a novelty.[41] The rebellion of the '20s assuredly left the youth disenchanted, only to find themselves getting further from God at an irrevocable rate.

41. Edley, vol. 3, 26.

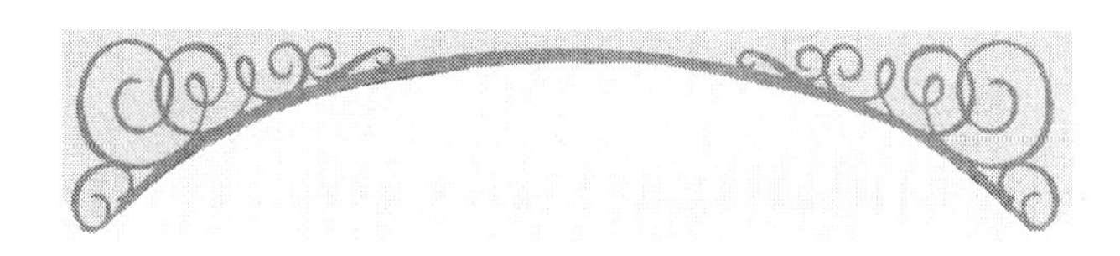

7 – Troubled Times Ahead

During the next couple of decades, it was as if the hand of Almighty God was totally withdrawn from America. The glory departed when the women of our country sheared their hair. Was it just a coincidence that troubled times came almost directly after women started cutting their hair, or was there a connection to the spiritual covering provided by obedience to God's Word?

We can apply the verse of Scripture, Deuteronomy 11:28, ***And a curse, if ye will not obey the commandments of the LORD your God, but turn aside out of the way which I command you this day, to go after other gods, which ye have not known.*** In I Samuel 12:15 is another exhortation warning us: ***But if ye will not obey the voice of the LORD, but rebel against the commandment of the LORD, then shall the hand of the LORD be against you. . . .***

The Lord removed His glory from our land when scores of women cut off their glory. The angels of the Lord were released from providing and protecting the American people. This stiff-necked generation turned away from the Lord in pursuit of fleshly lusts. As a whole, they lost their power over the enemy . . . so in came the troubles and trials of the fourth decade. The Bible says in Hosea 8:7, ***For they have sown the wind, and they shall reap the whirlwind. . . .***

Disasters Blow In

The whirlwind of disasters began to blow on October 24, 1929, when suddenly the stock market crashed. Pandemonium struck the stock market floor on that day. "Black Tuesday" cost the stock list over 14 billion dollars. Many committed suicide over the great crash.

Sherwood Anderson said, "The big world outside now is so filled with confusion. It seemed to me that hope, in the present muddle was to try thinking small." Most people were used to living "high on the hog," but soon they were reduced to just mere pennies. No more fun and frivolity, for their prosperity bubble had burst. The Book of Proverbs states, ***He that trusteth in his riches shall fall*** (Proverbs 11:28).

The Great Depression of the '30s brought multitudes to poverty. The richest nation on earth found out abruptly what it meant to be hungry, destitute, and bankrupt. Some 40 million people learned that this was becoming a way of life.

To add to the nation's burden of the depression, several natural disasters occurred. The flood of 1937 left over a million people homeless and in need of flood relief. The great dust storm that hit from Texas to Canada claimed the lives of many by suffocation. The drought destroyed hundreds of crops, leaving farmers virtually penniless. Unemployment skyrocketed. One family was known to have walked nine hundred miles just to apply for a job!

In hard times like these, crooks and gangsters took advantage of people. They were known to be carrying their sawed-off shotguns and Tommy guns. Mobsters like Dillinger, "Baby Face" Nelson, "Pretty Boy" Floyd, Bonnie and Clyde, "Ma" Parker and her boys, and Machine Gun Kelly were looking for easy money through robbery, kidnaping, and even murder. Looking back at this time, one could think that all hell was unleashed to wreck havoc and chaos in our nation.

All these tragedies happened in just the short span of ten years. Was it an accident, or was the Lord keeping His Word that when His people turn their backs on Him in disobedience, they are guaranteed to reap devastating results?

God has not left us wondering why these calamities might have happened, but He told us in His Word that they were for "a sign" for all to see. We find the Scripture saying:

> ***Moreover all these curses shall come upon thee, and shall pursue thee, and overtake thee, till thou be destroyed; because thou hearkenedst not unto the voice of the LORD thy God, to keep his commandments and his statutes which he commanded thee: and they shall be upon thee for a sign and for a wonder, and upon thy seed for ever. Because thou servedst not the LORD thy God with joyfulness, and with gladness of heart, for the abundance of all things*** (Deuteronomy 28:45-47).

It should be the hope of all Christians that their religious country will turn back to God. We are encouraged with the promise II Chronicles 7:14, ***If my people, which are called by my name, shall humble themselves, and pray, and seek my face, and turn from their wicked ways; then will I hear from heaven, and will forgive their sin, and will heal their land.***

During this time not all people were sucked into the riotous living. Revivals broke out throughout the country, for God had a remnant of people who loved Him and preached the gospel in spite of all the sin. As Romans 5:20 says, ***But where sin abounded, grace did much more abound.***

Grace Forges a Way

An elderly sister in the Lord told me her testimony of how she got saved in 1927 during the "bobbed hair" craze. Sister Annie Swank, seventeen years old at the time, was one of those girls who got her hair bobbed after the fad came out. The way she learned about the bobbed style was from the radio, newspaper, and magazine articles and advertisements since there was no TV in those days. She told me her sister-in-law was the one who bobbed her hair.

She thought she looked pretty good, you know, up with the times! She wore the makeup and jewelry to go with the new hairstyle. It became a god to her. She didn't want to go anywhere without being "decked out."

Sister Swank said one weekend she heard that a preacher, Rev. Smith was coming to town. He was the "Holy Roller, tongue-talkin' " type. She told me the people in those days thought tongue talking was of the devil. The folks in her town had never heard of this "Jesus Name stuff." Sister Swank said that people in her town of Leedey, Oklahoma, would throw rotten eggs and tomatoes at the preacher as he preached.

So she and four girlfriends went to the brush arbor so they could watch the "show" and see what was going on. Sure enough, the Lord began to convict her of sin. She repented that night, and God filled her with the Holy Ghost. But before she could get off her knees to leave, she said that the Lord told her to throw away all the makeup and jewelry and to quit cutting her hair. She told me she literally could not move her body until she made a commitment to the Lord. Finally, in a flash, she said "yes" to the Lord. She has lived for God all these years since.

She said the depression years were hard, but people would stick together, helping one another out. And the Lord provided the rest.

Deeper Decadence

As God did a work in the lives of many, our worldly nation during the '30s was getting worse and worse. Although sin has been happening throughout the ages, this was a time when people became blatant about it. Christian America began to split apart its people. Fundamental Christians were staying true to God and His Word, but the world was embracing its evil devices of the devil. The growing immorality of our nation couldn't be stopped.

The crowds were lured into the theaters. This became a relief for some from the somberness of the Great Depression. Instead of turning back to God, many turned to Hollywood that offered a temporary release . . . for a mere twenty-five-cent ticket. They sought escape from their despairing lives and found it in the glamour and glitz of the movie screen. Instead of praying as a nation, they got a false sense of security from the movie stars. In no time at all, many women adopted the hairstyles and fashions of the stars. This caused many citizens to grow more sensual and ungodly.

In 1932, German-born American actress and singer, Marlene Dietrich, not regarding the passage of Scripture in Deuteronomy 22:5, was first to been seen walking along the Seine River in France dressed in a man's jacket and pants. The Paris chief of police was outraged to see her dressed that way. He ordered her to leave. Soon, she was seen in nightclubs and on the streets in man-tailored pantsuits. In spite of all the giggles, it quickly started a trend. However, the trend in America didn't start until "Katharine Hepburn and Greta Garbo began wearing loose baggy trousers on the silver screen," says Lynn Schnurnberger in her book, *Let There Be Clothes: 40,000 Years of Fashion*.[1]

---

1. Lynn Schnurnberger, *Let There Be Clothes: 40,000 Years of Fashion* (New York: Workman Publishing, 1991), 352.

Preachers began to warn Christians of the evils of movies, as did the independent fundamentalist John R. Rice. He stated in his booklet, "What is Wrong with the Movies?" written in 1938, that evils associated with the movies are mostly the immoral lifestyles of the stars who become the role models and heroes in our society. They modeled the use of tobacco and were engaged in gambling, illicit sex, crime, impure love themes, and wearing ungodly clothing. Rice noted that the producers make movies for greed and notoriety, having no feeling of responsibility to society and morality. He said that they teach and encourage crime, endorse sin, teach and incite lust, break down virtue, and contribute to delinquency.[2] There was no stopping once the wild horse of immorality had been unleashed. In 1938, the growing attitude of society was expressed clearly in this poem written by Brenda Frazier,

I'm established now for '38
With the title of glamor and reprobate.
I've won a position in *Vogue* and *Harper's*;
For a hundred bucks I'll advertise garters.
I grit my teeth and smile at my enemies;
I sit at the Stork Club and talk to nonentities.[3]

The nation's time of troubles seemed to level off as some citizens adjusted to the lean years. Many were thinking that the new decade of the '40s would bring a fresh hope. But to their dismay, all eyes were upon the escalating tension overseas. The worst was yet to come for all in this fifth decade.

Germany had clamped an iron fist around Central Europe in the month of September 1939. Many history books tell of the tragic events that happened worldwide during this time. This book cannot list all the devastating events that occurred during World War II.

We must not forget that the ladies in Europe had shorn themselves, too, in the "Bobbed Hair Craze" of the '20s and '30s. They and all Europe were also going to reap results of catastrophic proportions.

2. Bernard, 145.
3. Edley, "Glamor Girl Serenade," vol. 4, 144.

The world was on the brink of holocaust, and just as the United States was gearing up for World War II, in 1940 RCA Victor came out with the infamous "radio-television." The programs were scarce during the war, but in June 1946, the National Broadcasting Company was ready to serve the American public. Soon, the TV became the newfound craze of the '40s decade, which became another sense of relief from the pressures of war. Soon, this new invention was found in nearly everybody's living room, which only drove the wedge further between so-called religious America and God Almighty.[4]

Ever since the onslaught of wickedness, our nation has never really made an attempt to get back to God. The decade of the '50s was just a time of regrouping from the war. It was a time of family togetherness, but many Americans still had the post-World War II jitters. They feared the threat of nuclear war from the Soviet Union. Some dug up their lawns to install bomb shelters. Many people started to report UFO sightings. During the decade of the '50s, there was an average of six hundred sightings per year.

Hollywood continued to spew out more ungodliness to further entrench America in its lusts. Marilyn Monroe and Elvis Presley, to name just a couple, became the modern-day "sex symbols," only to arouse a promiscuous appetite in the hearts of young people.

Many families became recreation seekers rather than churchgoers. America left the Rock of their salvation to embrace the upcoming "rock 'n' roll" culture.

The Angry Decade of the '60s

The '60s hit this country with a bang. This decade was known as the "Angry Decade." Bitterness and anger started with students rioting on the steps of San Francisco's City Hall in May 1960. Between 1964 and 1967, race riots rose out of control in 58 cities and left 141 dead and 4,552 injured.[5]

Once again the devil launched his wicked devices on the youth and

---

4. Allen, 415.
5. Edley, vol. 6, 148.

opened the floodgates of rebellion as had happened in the 1920s. The drug culture, the hippie movement, and the infiltration of Eastern religions all played a great part to further cause the decline of our religious America. This was the decade when we as a nation entered the post-Christian era.

In 1963 the infamous atheist, Madalyn Murray O'Hair, won the U.S. Supreme Court case *Murray vs. Curlett*, in which prayer in public schools was banned.[6] Thus, the "separation of church and state" started. This killed any protection against the evil influences in schools.

The sanctity of the home and marriage became the targets of the enemy's blows during the '60s. The devil slowly eroded the beauty of a man and a woman living in harmony as a married couple. Satan's assault caused a spiritual earthquake . . . shaking the foundational core of our nation.

As the sacred institution of marriage was challenged, a spirit of "free sex" began to entice America's youth. Many of the houses where kids took residence were called "communes." Free sex, psychedelics, and drugs were part of their modern-day living. This fad soon became an acceptable lifestyle. Couples all over the nation began to "shack up" with each other. And America, who once knew God, wallowed in the cesspool of fornication and adultery. Statistics show that divorces and sexually transmitted diseases began to skyrocket.

The nation was left stunned at the news of the assassination of its beloved President John F. Kennedy in November 1963. The nation left in a minor whirlwind shortly recovered with the confident L. B. Johnson assuming presidency. As he quickly took his place, however, he was hit squarely in the face with the Vietnam War. This war only fostered more protests, more bitterness, and more hatred in its citizens.

Soon, there was news of another assassination, that of Dr. Martin Luther King Jr., the country's foremost leader of the civil rights movement. The same year, while campaigning for the presidency, Robert Kennedy was assassinated in Los Angeles. These episodes caused despondency in the heart of the country.

In the spring of 1964, there was yet another invasion. A singing

---

6. "Madalyn Murray O'Hair," *American Heritage Dictionary*.

rock group "The Beatles" landed in New York. Soon "Beatle-mania" spread over a good part of America. Millions of young Americans were inspired to copy their style. Their over-the-ear, eyebrow-length hair started the long hair revolution that still haunts us.

By 1965 the crew cut was on its way out. According to one estimate, barber shops across America were being forced to close at the rate of one hundred per month.[7] A cloud began to settle upon society during this fit of rebellion that caused an interesting phenomenon, the blurring of the roles of the sexes. Thus, the unisex fashion was born.

The unkempt hairstyles of the men displayed their rebellion against "the establishment." As men began to protest against authority and the government, their shaggy, disheveled hair grew longer and longer. Some men's hair reached to their waists. Society in general gasped at the sight. Parents were dumbfounded and shocked as well.

Women, on the other hand, let their hair grow naturally, straight and uncut. They were known as the "flower children." "Love, peace, and happiness" was their motto, and "Turn on and tune out!" was the saying on the tongue of every young person.

The Eruption of the '70s

The '70s erupted with a bang as the New Wave–Punk Rock culture appeared on the scene. This kind of music was unconventional, rebellious, and emotionally charged. It pushed beyond the accepted boundaries of rock 'n' roll. Most of the music had decadent lyrics glamorizing drugs, sex, and suicide. It was the underlying emotional intensity of their music and not their musical talent that attracted listeners.[8]

The most notable event that shook this decade happened in the early part of 1973 when the U.S. Supreme Court declared abortion legal. Killing was done in the name of a "woman's right of privacy." From 1973 until 1995, over 30 million abortions were performed in the United States of America.

This number of deaths is 96 percent higher than that of the seven

---

7. Severn, 4.
8. "Punk Rock," *Grolier Multimedia Encyclopedia.*

wars the United States was involved in throughout our history. (The wars I refer to are the Revolutionary War, Civil War, WWI, WWII, Korea, Vietnam, and Gulf War.) Since December 1775 when the British Parliament declared war on America until the end of the Gulf War in 1992, the total loss of lives was only 1,160,374.

Punk Rocker

War's deaths do not compare to 30 million deaths caused by abortion in the first twenty-two years of its legality. Life that once was valuable to America is reduced to human garbage. Of course, they do not merely throw the fetuses in the waste cans any more but put them into incinerators or garbage disposals . . . to prevent the pro-lifers from retrieving them to show that the fetuses are human beings.

However, I heard on Dr. Dobson's radio program, July 1995, that in China they do the unthinkable. They do not throw away or destroy any fetuses; they . . . serve them as a delicacy in restaurants, supposedly to "enrich your health and give you a clear complexion." That, my friend, is the epitome of satanism and cannibalism!

God's holy ordinances are shunned by our newfound "do-your-own-thing" culture. America is continually rebelling in order to obtain the lusts of mankind. She doesn't want to hear what God's Word says. People will stop at nothing to make their "big bucks." They have a passion to make it "big."

In 1979 an accident at the Three Mile Island nuclear power plant brought near-disaster to the lives of millions. Many started to fear nuclear fallout. The microchip was invented, and a new world of computers was introduced.

During this decade the Farrah Fawcett look was the "in" thing. Everybody wanted to copy her shaggy, feathered haircut. The beauty shops started warning women to get the "dead ends" trimmed off their hair every six weeks. Until this time it was unheard of, and truthfully, it was just another money-making scheme like the hairstyles in the days of the bobbed hair trend.

The 1980s till Now

Once again in the '80s the TV became the avenue for more rebellion. Later TV became the highway to violence, murder, and pornography. In 1981 MTV became the craze for the young people. "Sex, drugs, and heavy metal rock-n-roll" was the motto for this generation. The computer became more fully developed, and now many are sure that the computer will usher the Antichrist into the world.

The '90s became the "environmentally conscious" culture, the age of recycle. Society cares more for the "mother earth" than for their souls. We had many natural disasters, floods, and earthquakes during the first five years of the '90s, yet many still have not repented. Instead of praying, many schools are teaching visualization, meditation, and all sorts of New Age gobbledygook.

The hairstyles today are outrageous. Some hairdos look so weird that one would think the person is from another planet. Youth dye their hair purple, green, or orange. They dress in all black, paint their fingernails black, and wear black lipstick. Some dye their hair jet black and wear it in a ponytail on top of their head.

There is a new "skinhead" fashion that may have been introduced in the late 1980s. This is where some young people shave their heads bald to associate themselves with gangs. I noticed the trend starting for the girls, too, in the '90s to shave their heads bald.

The women who do not shave their heads completely like to wear their hair short. They have no idea what the Word of God says regarding hair length. Unfortunately, the women from the '90s have such a situational ethics outlook that many don't want to hear what "thus saith the Word of God." Their spirit is one that screams, "You can't tell me what to do or what I can or can't do." If you ask them if they want the blessings of the Lord in their lives, they say, "Yes," but they are not willing to come under submission to His Will or Word.

A popular trend now is many of the teenage boys are wearing pierced earrings in both ears. The girls wear several earrings in one ear. They pierce their noses, lips, and eyebrows. . . . And I even heard of one boy piercing his tongue with a safety pin. He said it was there to keep him from speaking evil (a Hindu practice). I came across an advertisement in the yellow pages of our city's phone book. It was for "body piercing." Their ridiculous motto read: "Be good & you'll receive a lollipop." I've seen pictures of young people with the body piercing art (if you want to call it that!). It's the most demonic, hellish thing I've seen. Now the new trend I've seen in a magazine is torching your body. Instead of getting an ink tattoo, the kids use a blow torch and some kind of metal shape to brand a design in their flesh. The imagination of the devil is unbelievable. **How our country needs Jesus!**

Although there has been technological breakthrough in these past decades, never before has the world been out of control spiritually like this. One wonders, *Where is God in all this?* Sin is running rampant. Violence on our streets plagues the nation. Murder has now become the norm. Families are torn apart every day. There is an assault of rebellion, disrespect, and lawlessness.

The stage is set for the reign of the Antichrist. It has been said that now the leader of the feminist movement confesses that their movement has failed. The nation seems to have a desire to get back to basics, but it doesn't realize that this can only come by acknowledging our sins as a nation, seeking God with our whole heart, and turning from our wicked ways.

The Christian in a Pagan Society

My pastor recently said, referring to the onslaught of materialism, "In pursuit of the American dream, we have lost the Apostolic vision!" The decline of our religious America began at the turn of the century. Adults failed to tell the next generation "why" they believed what they believed. They lost their love for God, His Word, and His holy presence. America's spiritual deterioration continues to plummet as she seeks more and more ***pleasures of this life*** (Luke 8:14).

Through the recent decades, immorality has taken an even greater nosedive. Situational ethics is the norm. Now, we are to the point in America where right is wrong and wrong is right, where good is evil and evil is good. We are helplessly mixed up!

In I John 4:4-6, the Bible tells us, ***Ye are of God, little children,***

and have overcome them: because greater is he that is in you, than he that is in the world. They are of the world: therefore speak they of the world, and the world heareth them. We are of God: he that knoweth God heareth us; he that is not of God heareth not us.

This is where the confusion plagues some. They want to give ear to the Word of God, and give ear to the world. But you cannot mix the two; . . . it will never work. You simply cannot mix light with darkness. They are confused over trying to fit a square peg in a round hole. They want to be worldly and Christ-like at the same time.

This new millennium is a good time to tell all Christians that cutting a woman's hair is more than just a cosmetic decision; it's a spiritual disruption. Hair has been a symbol of rebellion for many generations. Christian women should not want to look like the world or fall prey to the world's lies. If we, the body of Christ, have a love for the world in our hearts, it will be easy for the devil to ensnare us and to defeat us in our spiritual quest. Then we, too, could possibly follow that downward spiral of degeneration and reap unwanted calamities. God forbid!

Deuteronomy 6:7 states, ***Thou shalt teach them diligently unto thy children, and shalt talk of them when thou sittest in thine house, and when thou walkest by the way, and when thou liest down, and when thou risest up.*** Let's not fail to tell our generation why women of God do not cut their hair. It's more than a mere conviction regardless of those who make it out to be nothing less than the "quirk of legalism." Legalism in its purest form doesn't offer any answers to the "whys." We will answer all those who ask why and tell them that the answer lies firmly in the Word of God. Many have disregarded its fundamental truths to follow their own lusts of the flesh.

A great number of women are not ashamed to humbly wear their "crowning glory" so that those who hunger and thirst for the Lord will be able to see us as different, set apart for God, a separate people from the worldly styles. We want the world to see His light shining through us. ***That ye may be blameless and harmless, the sons of God, without rebuke, in the midst of a crooked and perverse nation, among whom ye shine as lights in the world*** (Philippians 2:15). ***And we know that we are of God, and the whole world lieth in wickedness*** (I John 5:19).

Pentecostal ladies

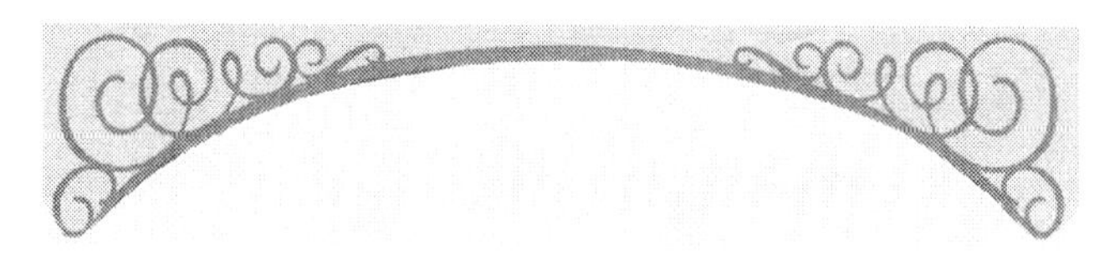

8 – Fun Facts about Hair

In this chapter we will discover some interesting and at times rather amusing facts about human hair. I will discuss the complexities of hair and its growth cycle. Then I will cover briefly how to shampoo your hair correctly and offer some solutions to the one troublesome area, split ends. Grey hair will also be discussed. Because the hair of each individual is different, the solutions mentioned here may not work for everyone. If that is your case, I recommend that you consult a hair professional.

This chapter is by no means the final authority on the techniques available to achieve healthy-looking hair. You can find some suitable books, by being selective, that offer very helpful tips for hairdressing . . . without adding any artificial means. The suggestions and tips offered by hair professionals worked for me personally and may be beneficial to you, especially if your hair is damaged. Much of the information given in this chapter is taken directly from hair care books.

Prelude to Beautiful Hair

Clearly anyone who has ever been tempted to think that a hair is a hair is a hair must think again. Hair differs widely not only in type, texture, color, and length, between different races, and between individuals of the same race but also on the body of the same person.[1]

There are some who are obsessed with their hair while others don't even think twice about it. Why, what's the fuss all about? At one time or another all of us have experienced our hair to be very unruly. It can become very frustrating. For guys, however, it is easy; they just step out of the shower, comb it a few times, and presto, are on their way. It is a lot more challenging, to say the least, with us ladies.

---

1. Cooper, 23.

I remember that when I was at Bible college several years ago, ladies were required to wear their hair up. I didn't mind that, but one day no matter what I did to it, my hair would not conform to any styling. Finally, in utter frustration, I called one of my instructors and told her I was not coming to school because I was having a bad hair day, literally. She laughed and told me that she'd see me the next day. It sounds funny—but not when it's your hair!

Hair can be your "crowning glory" when it looks terrific, or it can be your "worst nightmare" when you can't do a thing with it. I think that's why someone came up with the saying, "I feel like tearing my hair out." I heard someone say that God knew we ladies needed to work on our patience, so He gave us long hair. The best day in our lives is when our hair turns out nice for that special occasion. A nice hairdo not only will complement your looks but will make you feel better as well.

The Miracle of Hair

Jesus said in Matthew 10:30, ***But the very hairs of your head are all numbered***. The statement Jesus made shows His concern for even the tiny and seemingly insignificant details of our life. He is such a good God that He cares about the very minute things that interest us.

Hair is definitely an interest to us and possibly on the minds of millions of women. What God can number He can protect so that, according to Luke 21:18, not even a hair on our heads might ***perish***. And in I Samuel 14:45, God promised not one hair would ***fall to the ground***. While these verses of Scripture weren't specifically talking about growing hair on our head, He was talking about the promises of His protection. We cry out for His protection, especially when it seems that our hair is falling out by the handfuls. We worry, we panic, we pray, but we can be assured that there is a reason the Lord has created the shed cycle, which causes hair to fall out naturally.

Neil S. Sadick, MD, and Donald Charles Richardson state in their book, *Your Hair: Helping to Keep It*,

> The emotional impact of hair loss, combined with the loss itself, can actually create the conditions by which more hair is lost. Although worrying about hair loss

> does not in itself precipitate the loss, stressful situations such as operations, injury, acute illness, or severe emotional situations (such as the death of someone close) may exacerbate tendencies to lose hair in predisposed individuals. Both men and women who experience extreme stress about their scalp problems can suffer from diffuse shedding of hair beginning three to four months after a stressful episode. Stress may also play a role in precipitating alopecia areata, a disease of the hair follicles in which people lose well-defined patches of hair. This condition can show up as the loss of small patches of hair or, in its most severe manifestation, as total baldness all over the body.[2]

Authors Marion Mathews and Renske Mann state in their book, *Hair Magic*,

> From a purely functional point of view, hair is an immensely valuable asset. It is present on almost all warm-blooded animals and its purpose is to prevent heat loss from the body and to maintain an even temperature on whatever part of the body the hair grows. Hair covers the skull against the burning rays of the sun and to a limited extent gives a protective cushion against glancing blows and the risk of scratches and abrasions.[3]

In the July 1927 issue of *Hygeia*, authors F. W. Cregor and F. M. Gastineau wrote in their article, "Hair–Woman's Glory and Man's Despair," "It is believed that hair serves man as a preserver of heat and a protective covering and animals [have fur] as an organ of touch." The article continued, stating that the belief of Hilkiah Crooke, a physician

---

2. Neil S. Sadick, MD, and Donald Charles Richardson, *Your Hair: Helping to Keep It* (New York: Consumer Reports Books, 1992), 3-4.
3. Marion Mathews and Renske Mann, *Hair Magic* (New York: Arco Publishing, Inc., 1984), 17.

and professor of anatomy to His Majesty James I, in 1618, was "the one great office of the hairs of the head was to lead off 'the vapours which otherwise would choke, make smoaky the braine.' "[4] He did not mention how helplessly choked the brain would be if one were bald!

Hair can reveal a lot about us, especially our physical conditions. Through hair analysis, doctors can now detect vitamin and protein deficiencies. Hair and its condition can also indicate thyroid conditions, anemia, collagen vascular diseases like lupus, infections, infestations, and even AIDS.[5]

Fun Facts

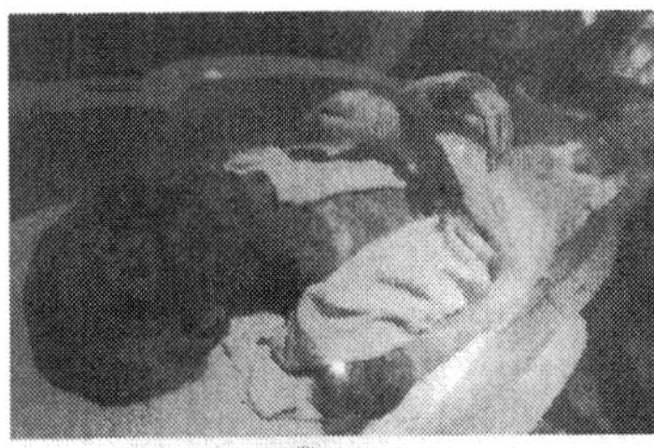

Hair is immensely durable, even after three thousand years. When the mummy of King Ramses II, who reigned 1279 to 1212 BC was found in 1881, experts were astonished at how well the king's body was preserved. With close examination, scientists determined that the king's hair must have been dyed with henna. Considering he is 3,260 years old, King Ramses II's red hair was amazingly still affixed to his skull. Many other royal mummies were excavated, as Queen Tiy, the grandmother of Tutankhamun. When Egyptologists found her royal cache in 1898, they noted that her hair had not deteriorated during the course of time.[6]

On March 16, 1995, I heard on the news talk radio program KGO from

4. F. W. Cregor and F. M. Gastineau, "Hair–Woman's Glory and Man's Despair," *Hygeia*, July 1927.
5. Sadick and Richardson, 4.
6. Putnam, 36.

the late Dwayne Gerritt that Napoleon Bonaparte's hair was sold at an auction for six thousand dollars. The talk show host did not say what they were planning to do with the hair. It seems like a waste of money.

Just for fun I decided to look in the *Guinness Book of World Records* to see who had the longest hair in the world. A lady by the name of Diane Witt of Worcester, Massachusetts, holds the record for the longest hair in the world.[7] When I checked the *Guinness Book* in March 1993, her hair measured twelve feet, eight inches. She last cut it in 1971. It grows at a rate of one-half inch per month. She takes four hours to shampoo it, possibly more. Normally, she wears it in a braid piled on her head and fastened with two hairpins.

On a whim one day, I decided to see if I could locate her. I wanted to ask why she kept her hair long and if I could obtain a picture of her hair to use for this book. I wondered if it was for any religious convictions or not. I left two messages on her phone.

Finally, one night she returned my call. She and I chatted for about thirty minutes; however, she was not at liberty to answer any of my questions. She made the comment that many people (e.g., Donahue and other talk show hosts) are wanting to get an interview with her, but due to circumstances she has not committed to anyone yet. Ms. Witt did say that her hair had reached thirteen feet as of June 1995.

The blessing in all this is that I did get to explain why I was writing this book, share I Corinthians 11:14-15, and tell her my testimony. Perhaps when she goes public I'll be able to ask all my questions, including: "How would you like to come to church with me to feel the presence of the Lord?"

A Hair Is a Hair

Each hair when added to the others makes up many hairs. A single healthy human scalp covers an area of approximately 130 square inches. The average number of hairs it has is one hundred thousand, but there are wide variations from this figure.[8] Blondes have as many as 140,000 hairs, whereas redheads have fewer than 90,000 hairs on their head.

7. David A. Boehm (ed.), "Longest Hair," *Guinness Book of World Records* (New York: Sterling, 1990), 20.

8. Cooper, 24.

Brown heads are somewhere between, averaging 108,000. Generally speaking, men's hair is coarser than women's. If we take a greatly magnified cross section of an average straight hair, we see that it is round in form. Curly hair tends to be elliptical, whereas Negroid hair is kidney-shaped and nearly flat on one side. Orientals' hair, which is always straight and round in form, is well supplied with oil, whereas in contrast, Blacks' hair tends to be dry. Blond hair tends to be fine, and curly hair is coarser.[9] Chemically, dark hair differs from blond hair in having more carbon and less oxygen and sulfur.[10]

"People with rich, full heads of hair do not have more hair follicles than Yul Brynner," says Jonathan Zizmor, MD, and John Foreman in *Superhair: The Doctor's Book of Beautiful Hair*, "but they do have better genetically inherited hormones that control both the quality and the quantity of hair on the head and body. . . . The people with especially thick, luxuriant hair may also have the following: 1) low levels of follicle-shriveling androgenic (male) hormones, and/or 2) follicles that are resistant to the effects of androgenic hormones by virtue of genetic inheritance, and/or 3) good levels of estrogenic (female) hormones that naturally counter the androgens, and/or 4) long and sustained growth cycles."[11]

Zizmor and Foreman's conclusion is "the essential quality of your hair is predetermined by your genes. You can't change what nature gave you, but you can cosmetically improve the hair you were born with."[12] It's a sad fact that not all of us were born with a beautiful head of hair, quite simply, because of what we inherited from our parents. But with a little time, prayer, and patience we can work with what God gave us. Hang on, and don't be too quick to grab the shears if your hair is not as luxurious as some. Wisdom says to work with what you've got.

I can remember, when I was a new convert, that I would be tempted to think that my hair was not as beautiful as other women. What I didn't know was that some of these ladies were growing their hair for

---

9. Mathews and Mann, 16-17.

10. Cregor and Gastineau.

11. Jonathan Zizmor, MD, and John Foreman, *Superhair: The Doctor's Book of Beautiful Hair* (New York: Berkley, 1978), 14.

12. Ibid.

years . . . sometimes ten, twenty, or thirty-plus years or more. The Lord said in Luke, ***In your patience possess ye your souls*** (Luke 21:19). And patience is what we need to carry us when we start growing our hair as new converts. Patience also is needed when we've known the Lord for some years, yet we're still struggling through those bad hair days.

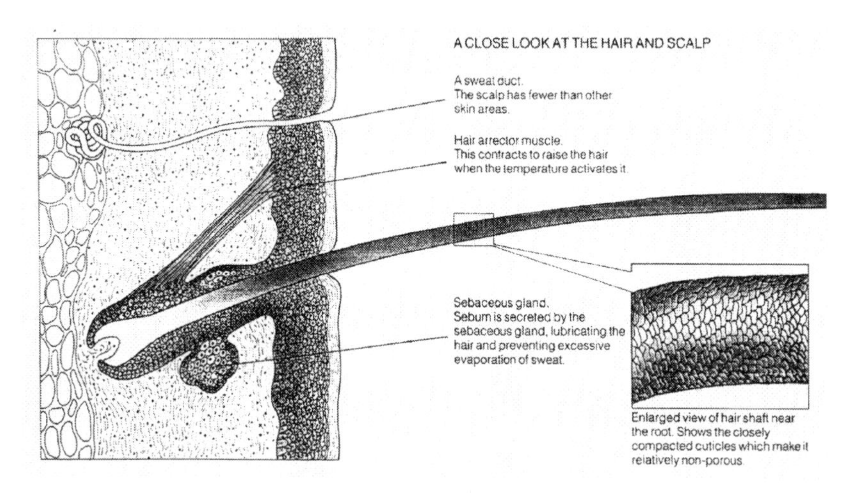

The unifying factors that all hair has, of whatever type, are produced from little pockets in the skin called **follicles**. The hair follicle can be compared to a "factor" with the actual manufacturing part, the **papilla**, as its bulb-like base. To think of the papilla as a "root" is a misconception. Even when a hair is plucked out, the papilla stays behind and starts making a replacement hair. The papilla is rich in minute blood vessels.[13] Each hair follicle is supplied by one or more sebaceous glands, which produces the natural oil to lubricate the hair. The oil produced by these glands gives the hair its gloss and richness.[14] Brittle or dry hair often suffers from a deficiency of sebum, whereas oily hair may result from an excess of it.[15]

---

13. Mathews and Mann, 16.
14. Cooper, 24.
15. Mathews and Mann, 16.

A hair lengthens only because a new piece of shaft is continually emerging from the papilla. This, in healthy people, occurs at a rate of about one-half inch per month, while in exceptionally fit people it can grow as much as seven or nine inches a year.

The hair shaft consists of three layers: the outer layer, also called the **cuticle**; the second layer, called the **cortex**; and the innermost layer, the **medulla**. To each follicle is also attached a special muscle, the **arrector pili**. Hair muscles can be seen working very obviously and dramatically on cats and dogs when fear or anger causes their fur to rise. In humans it is more normally a response to cold that causes the muscles to contract, producing goose pimples and upstanding hair. But in moments of great stress the same effect may be achieved through the body's hormone response. Our hair can stand on end with fear.

Reports from World War II, for example, tell of memory-haunted men whose hair stood on end for months after their experiences on the beaches of Dunkirk. A British army doctor, Sir Arthur Hurst, described such cases from the trenches of World War I in his book, *Medical Diseases of War* (1944):

> I saw several men suffering from the effects of severe emotional strain, whose hair permanently stood on end and could not be kept down by means of grease. In some cases I had the opportunity of comparing their appearance with what it was formerly, and the change from the sleek appearance when in civil life was most remarkable. One man, who kept his hair closely cropped, said his hair reminded him of the bristles of a hedgehog. . . . In some cases the hair of the body as well as the head has been persistently erect.[16]

In the Book of Job, Eliphaz stated, ***Then a spirit passed before my face; the hair of my flesh stood up*** (Job 4:15). When Job's acquaintance sensed a spirit near by, he, too, was frightened enough that his hair stood straight on end.

---

16. Cooper, 24.

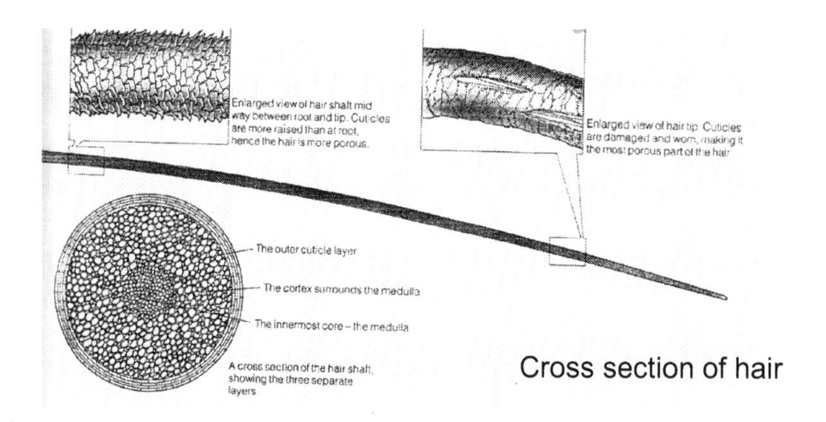

Cross section of hair

The cuticle is formed from tiny overlapping scales, similar to the scales of a fish or tiles on a roof.[17] If you have a microscope, find a hair that has fallen out in your brush, prepare a wet slide mount, and place it under the microscope to view the scales on the cuticle. I couldn't help it; I had to see it for myself. I discovered there are scales on my hair!

In the cortex, the second layer of the hair shaft, the hair's natural color matter, **melanin**, is found. The cortex comprises a great many long fibers which give the hair strength and suppleness. The fibers of the cortex separate readily and appear to be held together by the cuticle. Buried within the numerous fibers is the **medulla**, the innermost layer, made up of spongy, cellular tissue.

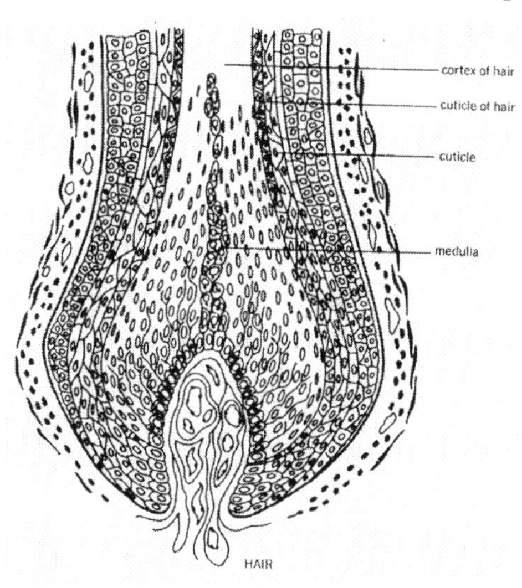

Length view of hair

17. Mathews and Mann, 16.

Within the medulla are very few melanin-producing cells to provide color. In very fine hair,the medulla is often absent altogether.[18]

If you want to feel the roughness of the outer layer, draw your fingers through the hair from end to scalp. It will give you a sensation of "going against the grain." Like fingernails, the cuticle is transparent and does not affect the color of the hair. When combed smooth, the hair looks soft and shiny, but when combed the wrong way, the hair can become dull and rough in texture. Improper handling of the hair and the use of harsh chemicals in dyes, perms, and shampoos can cause the layers of the cuticle to tear and loosen. When the hair is greasy, the cuticles tend to get clogged, thereby giving it a dull, lifeless appearance.[19]

The Growth Cycle of Hair

The growth cycle of hair is a natural yet mysterious phenomena that can better be described than explained. Every follicle is independent of another. In other words, each of the one hundred thousand hairs we have is mutually exclusive. Each has a three-part growth-and-shed cycle. The process is continued until eventually the life of each hair cycle stops. If it wasn't for the simultaneous growth-and-shed cycle occurring together, we'd all go bald periodically.[20]

Most hair specialists say that the hair-growth phases are staggered in a mosaic pattern. And thankfully so, because if the growth-and-shed cycle happened all at once, we would shed our hair and be bald from time to time. . . . It would be a ghastly sight! I can see it; if someone asked if we were going to church, we'd answer, "I can't. I'm molting!"

The way the Lord created us ladies (and men) is so the amount of our hair is growing continuously on our head at any given time. For men who go bald, experts say the follicles do not die; they just lie dormant. The current medical explanation for baldness is that accumulations of androgenic hormones in the bloodstream somehow permanently interrupt the continuity of the three-part growth-and-shed cycle.[21]

---

18. Ibid.
19. Ibid.
20. Zizmor and Foreman, 14.
21. Ibid., 15.

The first phase of the three-part cycle is called the growth phase or **anagen** phase. Rich in minute blood vessels, the papilla starts manufacturing amino acids that are synthesized into protein to feed the continuous formation of cells on the outer surface. These cells, continuously being created from below, push up the older ones, which, as they rise, undergo structural differentiation into the variously shaped cells that make up a hair shaft. After a final hardening process, called **keratinization**, the shaft emerges from the mouth of the follicle as a visible hair.[22] Just as your liver produces bile and your stomach produces digestive juices, so your follicles produce **keratin** that is the protein substance commonly called **hair**.[23]

If you deprive your bloodstream of essential proteins or calories due to an unbalanced and insufficient diet, your follicles won't produce good keratin.[24] This means that your hair is not nourished enough to keep it growing.

On the other hand, those who eat wisely and exercise will cause their blood to flow more rapidly and will produce richer keratin, which stimulates the hair to grow. According to the *Grolier Multimedia Encyclopedia*, "Hair gets its color from a pigment called **melanin**, which is made by cells called **melanocytes** and is responsible for all the colors of hair from yellow to black. Hair turns grey when the melanocytes die."[25] (More about grey hair later.)

The average rate of growth of a human hair for the duration of the anagen phase is only about a third of a millimeter per day. The length of each hair follicle's anagen phase varies significantly from one person to another, usually lasting somewhere between two and six years.[26]

The next phase is the **transitional** or **catagen** phase. This cycle is brief, perhaps lasting only a matter of weeks. During this period the catagen follicle winds down its rapid metabolism, wrinkles, contracts, and ceases the production of keratin. Catagen shrinkage is a natural part

22. Cooper, 23.
23. Zizmor and Foreman, 13.
24. Ibid., 14.
25. "Human Hair Growth," *Grolier Multimedia Encyclopedia.*
26. Zizmor and Foreman, 17.

of the growth-and-shed cycle and cannot be stopped.[27]

The final phase is called the **telogen** phase, which occurs when the follicle stops shrinking. This is a period of rest and suspended animation in which the hair does not immediately fall out but rather sits in the now fully contracted follicle bulb. The typical length of the telogen phase is around three months, during which the hair will rest in the follicle until it's physically dislodged by brushing or washing.[28] Normally, we lose anywhere from fifty to one hundred hairs from our head every day, and the life span of any particular hair is unlikely to be more than six years and may be as little as two.[29]

Contrary to a frequently held belief, neither shaving, trimming, nor cutting accelerates hair growth. This is just a myth. How could cutting the bottom of the hair make the top of the hair grow? The hair grows from the top and not the bottom; therefore, it is a false assumption to believe a monthly trimming will cause the hair to grow faster. Even if hair was not shaved, cut, or plucked, a hair still has only a limited life span before it falls out naturally and is replaced by a new shaft.[30]

This information is helpful to dispel any anxiety, particularly when we perceive gobs of our glory in the sink or at the bottom of the drain in the shower. Now we don't have to panic since we know it's a normal process of the growth-and-shed cycle. But, of course, if you still have your doubts and think maybe something else is going on, see a professional.

The Culprit's Temptation

Different types of hair suffer with many typical kinds of problems. This book will not cover the problems of oiliness, dryness, fragility, or dullness. If you have any of these hair problems, be sure that there are many suitable books to help you discover solutions to these common problems.

---

27. Ibid., 18.
28. Ibid.
29. Cooper, 28.
30. Ibid.

What is the culprit's greatest temptation to cut one's hair? Split ends are by far the number one culprit why ladies trim their hair. They want to get rid of those unwanted "dead ends." But according to most hair specialists, nine out of ten cases of split ends are self-inflicted. In the '70s, we called them "frizzies."

"Although the frizzies constitute perhaps the most common hair complaint," say Zizmor and Foreman, "the medical truth of the matter is that practically nobody was born with them. In almost all cases the frizzies are entirely self-induced by people who are unwittingly damaging the protective cuticles of their own hair, thereby allowing the softer inner structures of the hair in effect to unravel. . . . Patients with severe frizzies often complain, 'I can't understand it. I do so much for my hair.' That over treatment, of course, is usually the source of the problem."[31]

One of the biggest causes of split ends is overtreatment with chemical dyes, bleaches, and perms. Hair cuticles on various heads will tolerate the peroxide in dyes and bleaches to different degrees, but all chemical treatments will inevitably damage the cuticle. A ruined, ragged cuticle not only leads to split ends but also makes hair dull and difficult to manage. The worst scenario for hair is that it is dyed and permed together. In some cases it could damage the hair immensely.

Overmanipulation is another major cause of split ends. Everybody likes nicely styled hair, but overbrushing, overtreatment, too heavy brushes with sharp bristles, or excessive and careless use of brush rollers can all damage the cuticle or even deform the hair.

Too much heat is another culprit in the battle against healthy hair.

---

31. Zizmor and Foreman, 29.

Hot rollers, curling irons, blow dyers, and hot oil treatments are all okay in moderation, but overuse, especially of blowers, can literally scorch the cuticle. Once that cuticle is weakened, the hair shaft is inevitably going to split.[32] Split ends make your hair look ugly, according to some. But to us they are sacred ends.

The Lord knows how important a nice hairdo is to us ladies. However, some women go overboard. Unfortunately, they wrap their self-esteem around the looks of their hair like wrapping a piece of hair around a curler. You can't do that. It becomes dangerous. Self-esteem by definition is "good opinion of oneself" or "satisfaction with oneself." The Bible warns us in Romans 12:3, ***For I say, through the grace given unto me, to every man that is among you, not to think of himself more highly than he ought to think. . . .***

Self-esteem can only come from knowing we are saved and sanctified unto Jesus Christ. Most women don't have the trouble of thinking of themselves more highly than they need to, but the real problem lies in accepting themselves with what God has given them. And it's true, hairstyles can "make us or break us," but it shouldn't be at the expense of sacrificing our conviction to obey the Word of God.

The point of all of this is that cutting off your split ends is no cure-all solution, but taking good care of your hair is. You should try to eliminate abusive practices, which, at the very least, retard the rate of splitting. Do all the blow drying and curling in moderation. By this I mean: allow your hair to have a break from rigorous styling.

We can be thankful that we don't live in the medieval or Renaissance times. Many of those women nurtured their hair with all kinds of herbal medications. When that didn't work, they would apply dead leech skins to their scalp, which they believed to be beneficial in having healthy-looking hair.[33] Nowadays it is a lot simpler.

"While hair may survive, it does not always thrive," says *The Ann Landers Encyclopedia*. She continued:

> The abuse suffered by the average head of hair is incredible. Before thinning begins and split ends appear, something

---

32. Ibid.
33. Smithsonian Institution, 10.

> should be done lest woman lose her crowning glory. Beautiful hair begins with good health. It needs loving care and protection. What you don't know about hair care can hurt you. What you do know can mean the difference between having a magnificent mane and a dull, straggly mop that you'll want to cover with a scarf or a turban when you desire to look your best.[34]

The solutions to healthy hair are easy. First—be patient and calm down. Second, be kind to your hair and be sensible. And because we ladies do not spend a lot of money on cosmetics, I encourage you to use the money to buy some good shampoo products, not the ones at the discount stores or supermarkets. Buy the products from a beauty supply store. I've found that when I go into those stores and explain that I do not cut my hair and need a shampoo that revitalizes the natural keratin protein found in hair, they know just what I'm talking about and are willing to help.

I hate to say it, but for years I used to think that the people who work at salons were just salivating wolves lying in wait to cut my hair off. So I would never step inside those beauty places. But my scalp got dryer and dryer, until I desperately needed their help. The shampoo I used was drying my scalp terribly. The ladies I talked to were most helpful. Now I use the right shampoo, my scalp looks a lot healthier, and my hair has become twice as thick. It pays to ask around for help.

I heard a funny story on the Dr. Dobson radio program. A lady said that one day she was frantic for someone to help with her hair. Perhaps it was damaged—I really don't know. The lady went to the beauty salon, pleading with the hair stylist to do something with her hair. As she sat in the chair to get her hair done, she again pleaded for help. The hair stylist said, "Look, honey. This is a comb, not a magic wand!"

Some Simple Solutions

Some simple solutions I've found are: Before you shampoo, comb out tangles, preferably with a wooden comb (to reduce static), starting

34. *Ann Landers Encyclopedia* (New York: Doubleday, 1978), 522.

at the ends of your hair, working up to the top. When you shampoo, massage the scalp gently for five minutes. This stimulates the hair follicles. Avoid scrubbing your scalp like a man does with his short hair, or you'll probably get a lot of tangles.* If your hair is grey, don't use any amber or green shampoos. They have a lot of red and yellow dye in them and will turn your grey hair yellow. Use a clear or white shampoo, not a blue or lavender shampoo.*

Properly condition your hair; that is, apply conditioner to the hair from neck down, and use a small amount on the scalp to avoid overconditioning. If you rinse your hair with the coldest water you can stand, it will leave your hair shiny.* Never brush hair when it is wet; use a wide-toothed comb. Apply styling gel before you dry your hair to hold the curl in longer.

A friend who has hair to her calves (the model farthest right on the front cover of this book) told me to use a gel called "Just Long Hair" by the Roberts Corporation. This leave-in conditioning gel helps the ends from breaking easily, and it works great. Their detangler is also a great help to eliminate hair breakage. These products are explicitly made for ladies with long hair.

The days of combing your hair one hundred strokes are over; twenty-five strokes a day will do just fine. Any more than that may cause hair to break off or become oily. Use a soft, boar-bristle brush.* I just bought a paddle brush with boar bristles. It works great and feels wonderful on my scalp as I brush my long hair. Don't use cheap hair spray but use hair spray that conditions, not damages. If you've had a hairdo in for a week and there is a lot of hair spray, rinse it first with very hot water, apply conditioner first, comb out the tangles, then proceed to shampoo your hair.* This will reduce breakage from sprayed down rats, puffs, and back fluffs.

You'll be surprised at the difference in the results when a little extra time is given to your hair. After all, this is your crowning glory. As Nona Freeman once said, "Don't curse your hair; be thankful and bless it in the name of Jesus." Remember, ladies, above all else: ask the Lord to give you wisdom in treating your hair moderately and gently.

**Hair care tip from Sharon Grider, a Pentecostal hair stylist whom you'll meet in chapter ten.*

Grey Hair: Double Honor or Double Trouble?

The Lord promises us that He'll carry us through when we are old. Isaiah 46:4 says, ***And even to your old age I am he; and even to hoar hairs will I carry you: I have made, and I will bear; even I will carry, and will deliver you***.

Sooner or later, old age and grey hair come to all of us, sometimes with these perplexing questions: What are we going to do with the grey once it gets here? Are we going to gracefully accept it or go into denial and try to cover it up? What does the Bible have to say about grey hair? If it is so glorious, why do people dye it?

In the Book of Proverbs (16:31), we learn: ***The hoary head is a crown of glory, if it be found in the way of righteousness***. Many people have hoary or grey hair on their heads, but they do not walk in righteousness. So the sinner's crown is forfeited and it becomes a crown laid in the dust. . . . But if a person is found in righteous living, it's a glory to them. White or grey hair is the symbol of honor or authority, and it is entitled to respect.

Grey hair is mentioned again in Proverbs 20:29, ***The glory of young men is their strength: and the beauty of old men is the gray head***. The Word of God says that grey hair is beautiful, and those who have it are ***worthy of double honour, especially they who labour in the word and doctrine*** (I Timothy 5:17).

I can remember being taught respect for my elders as a child. In the eight years I went to parochial school, we would have to stand and greet the principal or teacher as she entered the classroom, chanting, "Good Morning, Mother Gemma." Today, if you go into a courtroom, all the people present are required to stand in honor of the judge entering the room. This shows respect for authority.

Perhaps the saying, "Respect your elders," comes from the Old Testament teaching found in Leviticus 19:32, ***Thou shalt rise up before the hoary head, and honour the face of the old man, and fear thy God: I am the LORD***. This is a lesson to the young to show respect to the aged. The Jews were taught by God to regard them highly. Those whom God has honored with the blessing of a long life ought to have honor shown to them. The godly and the wise are worthy of double honor. We are, therefore, obliged to adhere to good manners and respect for our elders; after all, that is what the Word of God teaches.

Clement of Alexandria said in his letter, "The Instructor,"

> And above all, old age which conciliates trust, is not to be concealed. But God's mark of honor is to be shown in the light of day, to win the reverence of the young. For sometimes, when they have been behaving shamefully, the appearance of hoary hairs, arriving like an instructor, has changed them to sobriety, and paralyzed juvenile lust with the splendor of the sight.[35]

Grey hair is a normal sign of aging that typically shows up in the fourth decade of our lives. But a person can inherit a gene to cause her to go grey prematurely. There are also medical conditions that cause greyness. If you lack vitamin B-12 or vitamin D, you may have a yellow complexion and your hair may be grey. Another condition is thyroid disease, which causes premature greyness. Some experience excessive greying when they have been through traumatic events. Though rare, there are cases of people "going white overnight." These people experience this as a result of emotional trauma or physical shock and perhaps need professional attention.[36]

---

35. Clement of Alexandria, vol. 2, 286.
36. Zizmor and Foreman, 77.

Although the white hair is rich in phosphate, sometimes the hair feels coarser than the hairs with color.[37] That's usually because of increasing dryness from a natural decline of scalp-oil secretions that accompanies aging.[38] The dullness can be cured by adding conditioner to replenish the natural oils.

What is grey hair? The grey hair is the process of decolorization in the production of hair. The color residing in the hair does not discolor. Even when hair is removed from the head, hair keeps its color for hundreds of years, so it is not correct to think that hair is fading.[39]

Why does hair turn grey anyway? Greying occurs when the body slows and eventually stops the production of color pigmentation in the hair follicle. It is the failure to deposit the melanin (coloring agents), which form in the cortex (center) of the hair in the base of the follicle and around the papilla.

As we age, go through stressful times, lack the proper diet and vitamins, or endure sickness or disease, the hair cells become less and less active. The cells have everything essential to produce a hair. The cells send out of the mouth of the follicle a hair, which, in a sense, is only partly completed. The melanocytes (melanin-producing cells) slow and eventually die, thus sending up a hair that has no color in it.

The term "grey" is not really the proper term for hair. "White" describes it better because "white is the absence of color." Hair has the absence of color. We only call it grey because it looks this way against the other hues in our hair.

According to Dr. Leon Augustus Hausman, a professor of zoology, Rutgers University, in his article, "Why Hair Turns Grey," which ran in the *Scientific American*, September 1925,

> After the hair leaves its papilla . . . above the surface of the skin, it is practically a dead structure. This is an important thing to remember. The hair's only connection with the body is that it is rooted in the scalp. It has no organic connection

37. Cregor and Gastineau.
38. Zizmor and Foreman, 77.
39. Cooper, 31.

> with the body. Neither nerves nor blood vessels run up into it. What is the significance? It means that no changes can go on in the hair after it leaves the surface of the skin. . . . Thus, after it has grown out beyond the surface of the skin, the hair cannot change its color any more than the outer garments which you wear can change their color.[40]

"Nobody knows why it [greying] happens," say Tony Ray and Angela Hynes. "As of right now, there is no way to stop your hair from turning silver once your inherited time clock starts ticking."[41]

It is the Lord's way of letting us know that we only have a few years on this planet earth to do His will. If we flounder through the decades, our grey hair is there to remind us that our time is short. Nothing is permanent. We need to get going, do something for God, and not waste the years.

For many, however, it's time to hit the panic button when the grey hair makes its debut. Because the grey hits around forty years of age, many go through what the psychologists term "midlife crisis." But the scientists tell us that the aging process can't be stopped. Along with grey hair comes the need for reading glasses, declining stamina, kids moving out of the nest, and the bodily aches and pains. There is nothing we can do about it, but many panic, regress, or go into depression.

The Works Of Josephus, "The Antiquities of the Jews," state, "Herod despaired to live much longer; and that, in order to cover his great age, he colored his hair black, and endeavored to conceal what would discover how old he was. . . ."[42] Jesus knew Herod dyed his hair, and perhaps this was why He made reference to changing your hair color as He was talking about oaths during the Sermon on the Mount.

Jesus said in Matthew 5:36, ***Neither shalt thou swear by thy head, because thou canst not make one hair white or black***. An oath

---

40. Leon Augustus Hausman, PhD, "Why Hair Turns Grey," *Scientific American*, September 1925, 307.
41. Tony Ray and Angela Hynes, *The Silver/Gray Beauty Book* (New York: Rawson Associates, 1987), 10.
42. "The Antiquities of the Jews," *The Works of Josephus*, William Whitson, A.M., (trans.) (Hendrickson, 187), 440.

guaranteed trustworthiness within the participating persons. The rabbis taught that oaths which omitted God's name could be broken and were not binding. They based this on the third commandment, believing false testimony consisted of taking God's name in vain and resulted in severe consequences. But Jesus maintained in this passage of Scripture that God is involved in heaven, earth, Jerusalem, and all things.[43] Our "yes" should be "yes," and our "no" should be "no." Thus, we should walk in complete honesty.

What does all of this have to do with aging grey hair, complete honesty, and dying hair? Jesus said we cannot make one hair white or black. Within ourselves we have not the power to change the color of our hair. But through the years, millions have been changing their hair color by artificial means, many to their own hurt. The dyes they used were very toxic and detrimental. We hear the warning against using those toxic dyes by church leader Tertullian in his letter, "On Apparel of Women,"

> The more old age tries to conceal itself, the more will it be detected. Here is a veritable eternity, in the (perennial) youth of your head! Here we have an "incorruptibility" to "put on" with a view to the new house of the Lord which the divine monarchy promises! Well do you speed toward the Lord; well do you hasten to be quit of this most iniquitous world, to whom it is unsightly to approach (your own) end![44]

Ancient Greeks concerned with the restoration of color to grey hair believed the application to the hair of a raven's eggs was effective. So potent did they consider the blackening ability of the bird's egg, that anyone submitting to the process kept his mouth full of oil, lest his teeth likewise be blackened.[45]

Again, Clement of Alexandria had this to say about dying hair, "Consequently neither is the hair to be dyed, nor grey hair to have its

43. Criswell, study notes, 1114.
44. Tertullian, "On Apparel of Women," vol. 4, 21-22.
45. Goodman, 253.

color changed."[46] Nonetheless, the people resisted. "The first-century Roman naturalist Pliny the Elder," says Charles Panati in *Extraordinary Origins of Everyday Things*, "wrote candidly of the importance of dark hair dyes. A preferred black dye was produced by boiling walnut shells and leeks. But to prevent graying in the first place, men were advised to prepare a paste, worn overnight, of herbs and earthworms. The Roman antidote for baldness was an unguent of crushed myrtle berries and bear grease."[47]

The twentieth-century woman, during the days of the bobbed hairstyle, increased the use of cosmetics and hair dyes. But in February 1928, an article in *Good Housekeeping* was titled "Shall I Dye My Hair?" The author, a physician, stated that the dyes used were inherently dangerous, containing toxic poisons. So the New York City Health Authorities wrote an amendment to the sanitation code of the city. The amendment was passed in 1926, prohibiting the use of "noxious hair dyes and cosmetics."[48] Additionally, Harding states,

> But hair, once grey, should never be dyed. Dyed hair makes the face look hard, and if there is one thing an aging face needs it is a softening frame. Grey hair is beautiful in its own color and its own right, just as maturity is beautiful if beautifully borne. Some of the most striking women one meets are the women with prematurely grey hair who have had fine enough taste to make the most of this so-called misfortune. They look as dignified and charming as ladies out of an eighteenth century court. Grey hair brings out all the delicate tones in the skin. It is striking, it is beautiful, it is never obviously artificial, as dyed hair almost always is.[49]

Even the beauty books of today are stating not to dye your grey hair. Ray and Hynes state:

---

46. Clement of Alexandria, vol. 2, 286.
47. Charles Panati, "Hair Styling: 1500 BC Assyria," *Extraordinary Origins of Everyday Things* (New York: Harper & Row, 1987), 232.
48. Corson, 616.
49. Harding, 164.

> I know some lucky women whose silver grows in beautiful streaks over their ears or in the middle of the forehead. Why would anyone want to cover this enormously attractive feature? Once your hair is more than one-quarter silver, I recommend that you try not to mask it. Your skin usually gets paler as your hair lightens. Your original hair color may now look too dark or have a hair "dyed" effect. Start reveling in your silver, and be proud of what it declares about you as a mature woman. Remember, youth is no longer the only game in town.[50]

One point brought out by Zizmor and Foreman is that coloring your hair "won't change your life, nor will it make you what you aren't. And if it's a matter for getting rid of grey, perhaps you should ask yourself if you don't really look more attractive with the grey."[51]

Even more, I like what Bernard states in his book, *Practical Holiness: A Second Look*,

> The Christian is to be content with the way God has made him. . . . Everything God creates is good, and we should not try to alter our natural, God-given appearance by using false colors for the face, false hair dyes, false eyelashes, or false hair. What is wrong with the complexion and hair we inherited? Why be ashamed of what we are? Why base our identity on the outward man? Why evaluate self-worth by physical appearance?[52]

We need not be ashamed of the complexion and hair God allowed us to inherit. Instead of pushing the panic button, we should resist the temptation to run and hide but accept who we are in Christ Jesus. Let's not fight nature but embrace her as a gift from God and give Him thanks for it. If there is truly something that is unsightly with our body, pray

50. Ray and Hynes, 10-11.
51. Zizmor and Foreman, 77.
52. Bernard, 162.

and ask the Lord to give you the grace to overcome.

Bill Gothard once said, "Our happiness is not dependent on our outward beauty but on our ability to experience the character of the Lord Jesus Christ. . . . If necessary, God sacrifices outward beauty to develop inward qualities, since our happiness is based on having these qualities."[53]

Our best reminder is found in the Word of God, I Peter 2:9, ***But ye are a chosen generation, a royal priesthood, an holy nation, a pecu-liar people; that ye should shew forth the praises of him who hath called you out of darkness into his marvellous light***.

---

53. "H." and "I.," Institute in Basic Youth Conflicts, textbook, 15-16.

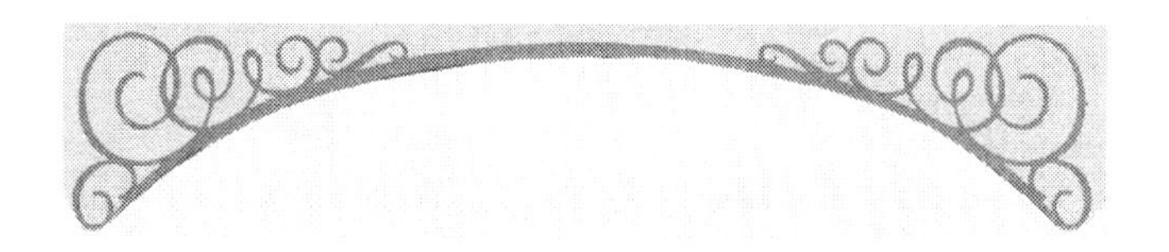

9 – Criminology and the Study of Hair

I never knew human hair held such a great significance to the criminologist and the forensic scientist. As I read my research material, I came across some interesting facts that stated hair played a vital role at the scene of a crime. To find out if this were true, I stopped to talk to a neighbor, who was a policeman who worked in homicide for years. I asked him if it was true that hair was an important factor if found at a crime scene. Officer Santos said it was "very true" since hair was as good if not better than blood or fingerprints.

Scientists can read DNA from the hair bulb and actually tell the difference between me or any other individual. That was enough to captivate my interest to search further, only to find a heap of intriguing information on criminology and the study of hair. Because of the complexity of the information, I tried to simplify the context as much as possible. Indeed, some of this material may be graphic for some; use discretion.

By One Fair Hair

Now we come to a brief yet fascinating part of our study. Throughout history, people have been intrigued with hair. Whether as a symbol of religious dedication or cultural status, it has played an important part in many societies. There is a flip side to the emphasis on the beauty of a full head of hair. "Societies have long shaved the heads of prisoners, traitors, or other lawbreakers as a mark of shame and punishment."[1]

A hair found at the scene of a crime could identify the criminal. At Limoges, France, in 1935, a mason, Pierre Bourget, was determined to be the murderer of an old spinster by just one fair hair left at the scene of the crime.[2] The microscope in the chemist's laboratory is one of the

1. Sadick and Richardson, 1.
2. Cooper, 34.

greatest tools for a forensic scientist so he can determine to whom the hair might belong. The swift art of detection aids in the conviction of a suspect.

Careful microscopic examination of hairs in a police laboratory will reveal characteristics of color, texture, thickness, appearance in cross section, and type of pigment, which all help in classification. Details of recent cutting, singeing, bleaching, dying, and perming that produce recognizable alterations can be detected. The Chicago police are reported to possess records of more than 150,000 different varieties of hair collected from criminals.[3]

Just from the study of a bit of hair retrieved from a crime scene, many questions can be answered. Is the hair from a human being or an animal? If it is human, was it from a male or a female? What is the approximate age and race of the person to whom the hair belonged? Was the hair pulled out, or was it cut? If it was cut, was a sharp or blunt instrument used?

An animal hair is easily detected when examined under the microscope. The hair of animal has a broader medulla than a human being's. The cells are shaped differently. The cortex, too, differs greatly in a man, and the cuticle of a human's is a lot finer than that of animal hair.[4]

The hair from a human scalp is particularly significant. Before the era of the bobbed hair, it was easy to determine the sex of hair. If the hair found was long and its tip pointed—uncut—it was most likely to belong to a female. Especially if the hair measured three feet long, it could easily be deduced that the hair most likely belonged to a woman, for in those days men generally had their hair shorter than women.

Nowadays, it is harder to be detected. Men wear their hair longer than what it used to be, and women wear their hair in a more mannish crop, close to their head. Scientists have discovered overall men's hair is usually coarser in structure and more wiry than that of a female. Generally, the hairs of a female are of a more delicate structure, contain finer granules of pigment, and less frequently contain a medulla.

The age of the person is determined by classification, stating

---

3. Ibid.
4. Goodman, 258.

whether the hair came from an infant, adolescent, adult, or elder person. The hair bulbs in age show degeneration, and the hairs themselves show signs of age other than loss of pigment.

Brian Marriner explains, "Hair plays an important part in a murder investigation. Because of its absorbent qualities it shows traces of poison, and analysis of the hair can reveal what poison has been used and in what dosage."[5] Because of hair's absorbing quality, arsenic can be detected in hair when no trace of it can be found elsewhere in the body.

The most famous case of suspected arsenic poisoning may be that of Napoleon Bonaparte, whose death on the island of St. Helena during his final exile, although officially ascribed to cancer, gave rise to rumors of foul play. In the 1960s samples of his hair were submitted to "neutron-activation analysis," and it was found, some hundred and fifty years after his death, that the arsenic content in his hair was about thirteen times the normal quantity.[6]

What is neutron-activation analysis? The elements present in any material can be converted into radioactive isotopes by bombarding them with neutrons. The elements can then be identified by the radiation they emit. This method is so hypersensitive that it is possible to detect and measure radiation from incredibly minute quantities of material. So it is now possible, though rather expensive, to identify the trace elements in hair that result from individual food intake, personal washing and shampooing methods, local pollution, and other environmental factors.[7]

"Whenever hair is collected for hair sample controls," states the Physical Evidence Bulletin, from the California Department of Justice, Bureau of Forensic Services, "the roots should be included because considerable information can be obtained. People may not like to have their hair pulled by another person. However, they generally can be persuaded to pull out enough of their own hair for root evaluation. The

5. Brian Marriner, *On Death's Bloody Trail* (New York: St. Martin's Press, 1991), 218.
6. Cooper, 35, and Marriner, 218.
7. Cooper, 35.

preferred method of sample collection is this order: 1) pulled hairs, 2) backcombed hairs, and/or 3) close cutting."[8]

Hung by Two Hairs

Through microscopic comparison the legendary pathologist Sir Bernard Spilsbury solved the 1930 Messiter case. Vivian Messiter was killed by a hammer blow from William Henry Podmore. On the face of the murder weapon Spilsbury found two eyebrow hairs from the victim. While this simply confirmed that this was indeed the hammer which had struck the fatal blow, the press headlined the case: "Two Hairs Hanged This Man."[9]

In Australia 1921, Charles Anthony Taylor, an industrial chemist, was involved in a murder case. The naked body of a young girl was found in a narrow street called Gun Alley. She had been strangled and bludgeoned to death. Detectives questioned people in that area and ascertained that the body had been dumped after 1 AM. The thirteen-year-old schoolgirl must have been killed elsewhere, then carried in a blanket of some kind and left in the alley. Logic indicated that the killer had to be someone who lived locally.

Police began to suspect a local shopkeeper, Colin Ross. All locals were questioned including Ross. Eyewitnesses placed Ross in Gun Alley at about the time the body had been dumped, one person even having seen him carrying a blanket-wrapped bundle.

Ross was arrested and questioned further. Two blankets from his shop were sent to Charles Taylor for analysis. The first revealed nothing under a microscope, but the second had twenty-one red-gold hairs extracted from it. Some hairs reached over twelve inches, which indicated a female. The hair had been pulled out by the roots; the shorter ones had been broken off. Microscopic analysis showed the hair to be of human origin, and the degree of pigmentation proved it to be of someone

---

8. "Collection of Fiber and Hair Evidence," Physical Evidence Bulletin, California Department of Justice, Bureau of Forensic Services, January 1986.

9. Marriner, 221.

thirteen years or over but under thirty, when coloring begins to decline. The short hairs came from the nape of the neck of a redhead. The victim was a redhead. . . .

The evidence of the hair counteracted any arguments of the defense, and Ross was found guilty and hanged at Melbourne Gaol, April 22, 1922—the first man in Australia ever to be convicted purely on forensic science.[10]

The Discovery of DNA Testing

The most dramatic advancement in the field of forensic science since the discovery of fingerprints is recombinant DNA technology. "This technolgy has provided the molecular tools that enable scientists to detect the extraordinary variability that exists among individuals at the level of their DNA (deoxyribonucleic acid). This will actually pinpoint the body fluid/tissue (hair included) to the donor to the exclusion of all other individuals," says Special Agent David Bigbee, Crime Laboratory Director Richard L. Tanton, and Bureau of Forensic Science Director Paul B. Ferrara, PhD.[11]

The DNA testing implemented in the forensic laboratories in the United States is able to analyze approximately ten thousand specimens per year. The FBI laboratory is currently spending approximately eight weeks from start to finish for each case. The DNA unit has more than five hundred cases awaiting analysis.

According to Ed Timms and Steve McGonigle in their article, "DNA Tests Prove Useful to Defense, Prosecution Alike," which ran in the *Dallas Morning News* April 11, 1993, "DNA is the genetic blueprint found in every cell of the human body. Except for identical twins, no two people have the same pattern. Identifying a 'match' typically requires a comparison of blood, saliva, semen, skin or hair samples and a complicated statistical analysis. . . . The chance of someone whose

10. Ibid., 221-224.

11. David Bigbee, Special Agent; Richard L. Tanton, Crime Laboratory Director; and Paul B. Ferrara, PhD, Bureau of Forensic Science Diretor, "Implementation of DNA Analysis in American Crime Laboratories," notes given by Officer Bill Santos, SJPD.

DNA pattern matches another person's sample could be one in 100 million, for members of a large ethnic group."[12]

DNA Testing of Hair Collection

Tribute was given to the dedicated detective work and the forensic scientists involved in a Florida murder case. Sharon Zellars, aged nineteen, disappeared as she drove home from work at Disney World, December 30, 1978. Her worried parents notified the police, and an air search was conducted, only to find her car abandoned in an orange grove. Bloodstains were visible in the interior of the car on the driver's side, together with a purse. Dusty shoe prints were found on the interior of the car, which revealed that they came from a military-type pair of boots.

The car was meticulously examined at police headquarters. A single strand of hair was found at the base of the seat belt attachment on the passenger side. A further search revealed several more matching hairs. The car interior was carefully vacuumed and samples collected.

On January 5, 1979, the body of Sharon Zellars was found in a well about fifty feet from where her car had been left. Signs showed she'd been battered to death. Routine detective work revealed that on the night Sharon was murdered, a guest at the nearby motel had sent for an ambulance. He had been bleeding profusely from the mouth and claimed he had been in a fight at a nearby skating rink, where he received an uppercut and bit his tongue.

The hospital doctor who tended to the man said the patient had lost about three-quarters of an inch from the front of his tongue, which had been bitten off. Security guards at the skating rink were adamant that there had been no fight on the night in question. A nurse at the hospital, who had treated the man's wound, said he could not have bitten off his own tongue—the curve was in reverse to his bite. The conclusion was that the victim had bitten it off. . . .

---

12. Ed Timms and Steve McGonigle, "DNA Tests Prove Useful to Defense, Prosecution Alike," *Dallas Morning News*, 11 April 1993, vol. 5, art. 9, 1A.

Meanwhile the suspect, Robert C. Cox, had returned to his military unit in Georgia, thus moving effectively out of the police hands. But the detective in charge of the case was not to be deterred. He examined Cox's service records, finding that he had a history of attacking women. Any questioning of Sharon Zellars was denied by Cox. However, the police got court permission to take hair and blood samples from him for possible DNA testing—then in its infancy stage in the US.

Seven years later, the detective wanted to contact Cox again, but he discovered that Cox was in prison, serving nine years for attacking two more women. In January 1988 the car blood residues were delivered to the Cell Mark Diagnostic Laboratory in Maryland, which was carrying out the DNA testing. The result was disappointing. The lab reported that there had not been sufficient DNA material to make a test. But the McCrone Associated Inc. Laboratory in Chicago had more luck with the hair samples and was able positively to match the hairs found in the seat belt of the victim's car to the head of the suspect.

On June 27, 1988, Cox was convicted of the murder of Sharon Zellars and sentenced to death. He now resides on Florida's death row. This case was one of many that made a breakthrough in DNA testing.[13]

The significance that hair holds for a detective has become greater with the use of DNA testing. The experts predict that DNA evidence not only will become routinely used in prosecution criminal cases but also will be employed with increasingly powerful effect. New technology and analysis, scientists say, will dramatically improve the ability to identify a suspect through DNA.

Already, some prosecutors say, just the threat of a DNA test helps boost the number of confessions and pretrial plea bargains. "As an investigative tool, it's working great," said Mr. Levy, the Tarrant County prosecutor. The ability to exclude potential suspects, he said, helps police focus on finding the real culprit.[14]

---

13. Marriner, 231-233.
14. Timms and McGonigle.

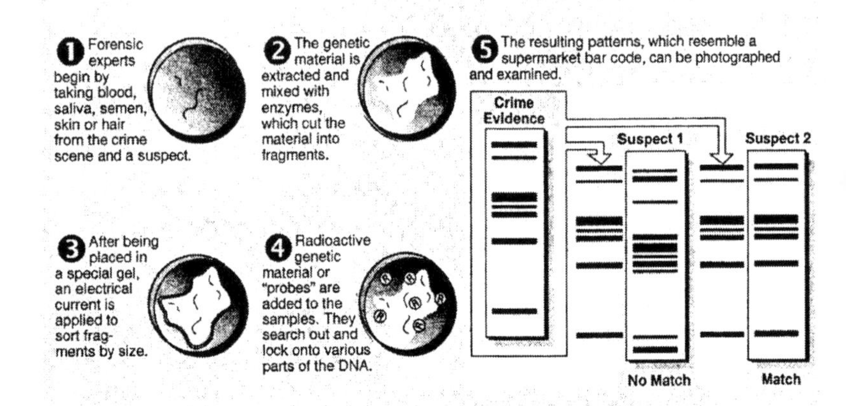

How DNA identification works

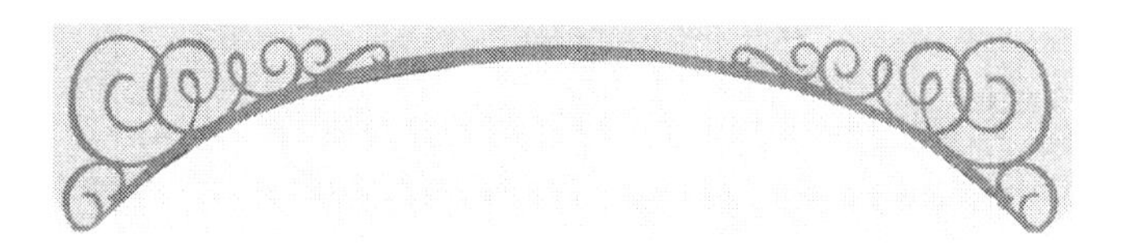

10 – Sacred Ends

In 1856 Andrew McNally and his partner William Rand founded Rand McNally & Company. Their specialty was making comprehensive atlases that individuals all over the world could understand. In doing so, they adopted a simple credo: "Fit up for a Specialty and Stick to it." In other words, find something that's worth sticking with until it becomes to you a specialty. By sticking to the subject of hair and spending over two years of research so that I could give an answer to whether hair has significance or not, I feel that it has now become a specialty for me.

Alexander the Great dreamed that he would conquer the world, and at the age of thirty-three, he died with no more world to conquer. When he was asked how it was that he conquered the known world, he replied, "By not delaying!" Although the motto of Alexander the Great is simple, there's a lot of truth to it. When it came to organizing and recording all the information on hair that laid before me, it looked overwhelmingly impossible. But as I read the account of Alexander the Great, I felt the surge of urgency and resisted from delaying any further.

The time is right to conquer any spirits that would try to snuff out the "glory" of the church. Hopefully, this book has assisted you in clearing any confusion that might have spread in our minds about the woman's glory. The world would try to tell us that our split ends "must" be cut off in order for our hair to look presentable, but I say no matter how jagged the ends of our hair might appear, they are "sacred ends."

Now that we reach the closing of this book on hair, there might be those who still wonder if there are any women left who still believe in I Corinthians 11:6, 14-15, or they may wonder if the Scripture has any significance. Many have said to me, "Just take a look around you and see how many ladies are cutting their hair." Some ladies are not adhering to the will of God by keeping their hair in its natural state. This may be true, but let me offer some encouragement.

If you have been despondent about that very thing, I assure you that a host of ladies believe and adhere to it. They plan to continue to stand firm on His Word no matter what the world dictates. Along with our heart, soul, and spirit, we have dedicated our "glory" to God. He will give us wisdom to treat our hair with the dignity that God intended it to have, not in a spirit of haughtiness but ***a meek and quiet spirit, which is in the sight of God of great price*** (I Peter 3:4).

Here are some pictures of "sacred ends" to indicate to the world that we are not ashamed but are grateful for His grace and mercy toward us. These women are happy to display their glorious tresses, which flow down their backs, that is their sign of submission to the Lord.

Some very sacred ends

Summary

We learned in the previous chapters that there is great significance to the subject of hair. In the supernatural realm, hair is believed to have been endowed with mystical and magical power. In the biblical aspects, hair was used to specify status and denote identification. In criminal investigations, it is used as evidence that may be tested to convict or dismiss a suspect.

Throughout history hair has been also the most revealing and important part of the human body in terms of social, spiritual, and psychological significance. It was used to set fashions and to adapt a means of attracting attention.[1] In some incidents, hair was used historically to portray an attitude of rebellion against the establishment.

For the individual not intending to make a statement with his or her hair, the condition, appearance, and particularly, presence of hair maintain a distinct mystique that is every bit as fascinating and influential today as it was thousands of years ago. If there is still any doubt in your mind that contemporary society places a high value on hair, simply leafing through newspaper or magazine articles and advertisements will show you how important hair is to the general population.[2]

Do Hairdos Make a Difference?

A favorite story about hair was told to me years ago in Bible college. Rev. Wayne Trout, pastor emeritus of Kent Christian Bible College, loves to tell this story to the students and nearly everyone. One day Rev. Trout and his wife, Sister Janet Trout, were on an overseas Holy Land tour. She, like most Pentecostal ladies, wore her hair up, on her head and styled nicely in a back-fluffed fashion. That day she decided to wash her hair.

The first thing one must do before shampooing is to take down the existing hairdo and comb out all the snarls before washing. Just as Sister Trout took her hair down and was combing it, there was a knock at the

---

1. Mathews and Mann, 11.
2. Sadick and Richardson, 2.

door. Perhaps pressed for time and annoyed at the interruption, she answered the door with her hair looking like she had gone through a wind tunnel.

Who could it have been? None other than Rev. Lee Stoneking. The part of this story that Brother Trout likes to emphasize is that Brother Stoneking is not married and possibly not used to seeing women (Pentecostals) without their hair fixed up nicely on their head. When Brother Stoneking saw Sister Trout with her hair blown out of proportion, he gasped and said, "Hairdos *do* make a difference!"

The moral to this story is that we ladies have known for a long time that hairdos do make a difference. That's why we toil over our hairdos. It is real work getting a hairstyle that is becoming to our features. We know what charm or repugnance we can bring to our faces by the sweep of a comb. As someone said, "Clothes make a man, and hair makes a woman!"

An Alfresco Toilet (1889)

Generally, hair has been a sign of our physical condition and how we perceive ourselves. It shows our personality, individuality, and imagination. Hair can be used to transform us by altering our features or concealing our defects. Our hairstyle can make us look younger, taller, prettier, softer, stronger, wiser, or more attractive.[3]

Sharon's Story – The Day I Lost My Glory

Sharon Grider has been a Pentecostal hairstylist for more than thirty years. Through the many years of styling hair, she has probably

3. Smithsonian Institute, 5.

curled, twisted, knotted, tied, combed, washed, waved, woven, braided, plaited, straightened, fluffed, ratted, heated, and finally sprayed her work of art to help innumerable Pentecostal women to look their prettiest. Thankfully, she dedicated this God-given talent to the Lord at an early age.

She was intrigued with Pentecostal women's long hair since she was a little girl. She remembered her first spanking when she was two or three years old for playing with her mother's friends' hair. Sharon was a preacher's kid, and in her home it was normal for visitors to drop by. That was her favorite time. She couldn't wait for the ladies to come over so she could give them a hug, then play with their hair.

Sharon remembers as a little girl she would climb on the couch trying to get to the ladies. Her mother constantly instructed her not to try to mess with the ladies' hair. Many times when her mother knew that ladies were coming over to the house, Sharon would be warned not to attempt to play with their hair, but to no avail. She would somehow work her way next to a lady, with a comb hidden behind her back.

In those days women would wear their hair in hairnets. The front was styled in pin curls. Ladies wore a wave pushed forward to the front of their head. Many times during the '50s, if the ladies wanted to give height to their hair, they would fluff it in a bouffant style. They would save their hair that fell out in their brushes and combs and use it as a filler. Sometimes the hair was stored in a jar or container. Sharon remembers it vividly . . . because she used to get into the jar and play with it. That would lead to a scolding from her mother. Sharon said she ruined many dolls by combing and combing and combing their hair. Her first hairstyling episode ended up with a good spanking.

A lady came to Sharon's house one day. Finally, after much pestering, she allowed Sharon to play with her hair. She could remember the ecstatic feeling coming over her. But being very young, she proceeded to wrap the hair around and around the comb. Then she tied the ends in all kinds of knots. After her mother discovered what she did, Sharon got a good spanking for it.

Sharon thinks that her interest with long hair probably came from the fact that her mother and grandmother had very short, uncut hair. Their hair was the type that wouldn't grow. When someone who had long hair would come to the house, Sharon would become very fascinated and enthralled. As she marveled at its beauty, she yearned to play with their hair!

When Sharon was six years old, her father felt the call to the mission field. They moved to Monterey, Mexico. In 1960, while on furlough in the United States, Sharon and her family were driving in the desert. Suddenly they got into a severe accident, which took the lives of her father, brother, and sister. Her mother was severely injured; Sharon suffered third- and fourth-degree burns on 65 percent of her body.

At the age of eight, Sharon experienced the horror of losing all her "glory." After the accident, Sharon ended up in the hospital seven and one-half months. During the long stay in the hospital, none of the nurses knew how to care for her long hair. It turned into a matted, tangled mess. There was debris still stuck in her hair from the accident.

A month later the nurses took it upon themselves to cut her hair. That was their "only" solution to her matted hair. They really did not know how to cut hair. She said it looked hideous. After she was released from the hospital six months later, Sharon's mother took her to a beauty shop to have her hair cut properly so that, at the very least, her hair would grow out evenly again. She remembers to this day the disheartening feeling she got. She says it was as if she had lost an arm. She looked on the floor at all her hair laying there. She just wanted to bundle it up and save it. That must have been an awful feeling to see your much treasured "glory" lying in a heap on the floor at the beauty shop.

Sharon recalls that during the time of recuperation she was not a very active child. She was confined to a wheelchair and later to the house in general. So she would sit in front of the mirror, practicing combing her new, growing hair.

At the age of nine, she loved to go to church and ask the ladies how they fixed their hair. She said she wanted to know all the details of their hairdos. She would go home and brush her doll's hair in the same fashion. But her mother would complain that all Sharon wanted to do was to play with her doll's hair!

When Sharon was a teenager, she received many compliments on the hairdos that she did. One day her pastor made a comment in church that all the ladies looked lovely. Then he said it was primarily because of another young person who fixed their hair. He told all the ladies that it was time Sharon got paid for her efforts. This is how her Pentecostal hairstyling career started.

At the age of seventeen, she fixed all the bridesmaid's hair for a wedding. The girls later decided to go to a restaurant. An affluent man there saw the hairdos of the girls. He was astonished that it was a young girl who did them and not some professional. He proceeded to offer Sharon a very lucrative job in Los Angeles, combing wigs in one of his beauty salon chains. But it was too late because, a month prior, she had dedicated her God-given talent to Jesus for His service.

I asked Sharon to describe some of the Pentecostal hairdos of the past. Every time I'd ask some of the old-timers to describe some of the "dos," they would just smile real big. One brother said, "Sister, you don't want to know." After talking with Sharon, I think I know what they were talking about. For those of you who don't know, however, here is what it was like.

The good ol' days?

The hairdo in the '60s was somewhat influenced by the world's styles. The Beehive and the French roll were then the popular thing for the Pentecostal women; for younger girls it was the ponytails. Some of the ladies wore a half-shell or half-bun on the crown of the head.

The '60s and early '70s were the time when the stories came about of women shouting out various items from their hair. During the church services or the altar services, Sharon remembers it to be a fascinating time because you'd never know what you were going to pick up around you after altar service was over.

Sharon named some of the things women used in their hair. These were the things she saw as a young girl (It may sound like "Ripley's Believe It or Not"): hairpieces (wigs), yarn (same color to match the lady's hair), toilet paper rolls, hair fillers, nylons, bridal netting, cotton batting, and the last one, I couldn't believe it . . . feminine napkins!

It must have been quite a sight! Later in the '70s, there was a new product of crepe wool that was used to achieve the same bouffant look. Then in the '70s "perms" became the popular trend . . . until some ladies, Sharon commented, abused the perms to shorten their hair. This made a possibly good thing turn into something bad and disgraceful.

Women did things to their hair that deliberately damaged it and made it shorter. One example I remember when I got saved in the late '70s is that some women called "perms" a "Pentecostal haircut." They knew that the perm would make their hair break off, so they would continuously get perms in their hair for that specific reason. One lady Sharon knew hated the fact that she "had" to grow her hair long because she was raised in the church, so she permed her hair three times in one week, leaving the chemicals on long enough to damage the ends so they would break her hair off. Perms might have been a good thing if they weren't wrongfully used.

Glory Lost Again

During this time, Sharon's hair grew from her waist to mid-calf, which was unusually fast for three years (1976 to 1979). Then in October 1979, she got phlebitis. When the doctors looked at her, they found three golf-ball-sized blood clots in her right leg. She was immediately hospitalized and was put on intravenous feeding. The necessary blood thinners, heparin and coumadin, had adverse side effects—severe hair loss.

After two weeks' treatment, as she was ready to go home from the hospital, her scalp began to tingle, and it felt as if it were crawling. Sharon describes her scalp as tightening; then her scalp would relax. Sometimes she felt a ticklish sensation on her head. She noticed hair lying on a pillow that had fallen out of her scalp.

After a month of follow-up treatments of blood thinners, she could remember the feeling of panic coming over her as she put the brush to her head. As she pulled the brush from her scalp, the bristles were packed with hair. It seemed like gobs of her "glory" were falling out. Swiftly was Sharon plagued with the memories of her mother losing her hair to chemotherapy. Fear began to run rampant in her mind.

By early 1980 Sharon had a very painful bald spot in the back of her head. She describes the pain as burning. She said that it hurt even to cover it with existing hair. As her long hair fell out, she could see the short, newer hairs trying to grow back in.

Sharon could remember seeing this happen to a few other women when she was a teenager. First, their hair was long, but then they said it got shorter by a severe case of stress. But in her immature teenage mind, Sharon really thought, *Uh-huh. Sure, it was stress. You are just using that as an excuse. Does that really happen?*

But now that this was happening to her, she wanted to scream louder than anyone around. All she wanted was for her hair to stop falling out. The doctors said they couldn't help her. But they just didn't understand that this was her well-beloved "glory."

Her pride got in the way and said, "This can't happen to me!" But it did. She learned that just as she judged those poor women suffering from hair loss when she was a teenager, she too, was going to be judged. Sharon realized that it would be impossible to go around explaining to everybody that her short hair was new growth. It was not this way deliberately, but it was because the hair kept falling out. Her hair was once mid-calf, but now it was near shoulder length. God was helping her to learn how to be gracious to those people who still chose to believe differently (and wrongly).

The new hair mixed with her longer hair caused a matting. All the new hair was finer and thinner. Sharon was going through a very stressful period due to several losses about five and one-half years ago. Her hair began to fall out again.

Then just lately, more stress came her way, but this time when her hair fell out, it never grew back any new follicles. Her hair was so thin that you could see her scalp. She thought she was going bald.

Thankfully, Sharon knew how to style her hair in a way so it didn't look so thin. She made her hair look like it still had some fullness to it. Although her hair was short—shoulder length—Sharon has a conviction not to style her hair in a way that looks worldly or that makes her look like she is of the world and not Pentecostal.

Sharon has a friend whose mother taunts her about looking like Pentecostals. She asks, "Why do you want to look like those women?" In other words, why identify yourself with the way those women look?

The answer is simply because we are all part of God's family. And it just so happens when you grow your hair long and it reaches to the waist, there are only a few ways you can wear it. Therefore, it seems we all look alike. That's why our hairstyles and the hairstyles prior to the era of the bobbed haircut in the '20s look very similar.

Sharon makes a very good point that if one works at a place that requires you to wear a uniform, you are not going to argue with the boss to wear blue jeans. She says if you are in the army, you're not going to wear a navy uniform. You want to look like the group you are a member of. You conform. You agree to look and to dress as their standards call for. Restaurants, airports, and hospitals all have their own dress codes and ethics.

It's a wonder why a Christian woman would not want to look like a dedicated child of God. Sharon states that she has trouble with understanding why some Pentecostal women don't mind "being" Pentecostal, but they don't want anyone to think that they "look" Pentecostal.

Sharon has the ability to comb her six-inch hair in a style that looks like a worldly fashion, but she doesn't have those kind of styles from the world in her heart. Some have asked her why she doesn't let her bangs hang down to make herself look younger or cuter. You could hear the sincere cry of her heart by the tone of her voice; she said, "I just want to look Pentecostal." With her hair, once long and thick, now short and thin, Sharon said it has become one of the biggest struggles in her life that has been consecrated in a bath of tears.

Conclusion

After reading this book, someone may wonder if all she has to do is just let her hair grow long and everything will be all right. No, that's not how it works because we must serve the Lord with our whole mind, body, and spirit. Really, what is in a person's heart will manifest in her body (appearance) and spirit (actions).

If a lady has long, long hair but has a heart full of bitterness and strife, the spirit of godliness and holiness cannot shine through her life. On the other hand, if a woman is working for God as a Sunday school teacher, an intercessor, or, for that matter, a minister and has not the spirit of godliness and holiness in her appearance, how can the world tell that she is any different from them?

One time, I wanted to get involved with the community college Bible club. Before I found out any information about the Bible club, I saw a woman passing out literature in the courtyard. By the looks of her hair and the way she was dressed, I thought she was lesbian. As I passed her, I noticed she was handing out brochures, but I wasn't interested. So I quickly walked by. Unbeknownst to me, when I found the meeting place of the Bible club, there was that *same* lady. . . . She was the director of Bible club. I couldn't believe it!

I was told by Sharon that there have been plenty of people who have come up to her through the years to make comments about the Pentecostal women. Those who commented don't go to her church. They said, "The women in your church are all so pretty. They just have a beauty about them. I don't know how to express it; they look so well groomed and neat. The ladies have such a radiance about them." I told you that story not to toot our horn but to let you know that the world can see the difference.

I'm glad that I'm different from the world but not for "the sake of being different." I'm just happy that the world can see there is a difference in my life because of Jesus Christ and His precious blood. The power of the Holy Ghost has greatly changed my life. I was meshed in the world's ideology and standards, but, thank God, I'm now free from that junk.

I read something this year in the *Pentecostal Herald* that deeply touched my heart. I want ladies to know that there are others who also believe there is significance to the ladies' hair. So I close with this. . . .

One Final Word

The final word is yielded to our honorable [late] General Superintendent Nathaniel A. Urshan. He stated recently in his article, "Hearing the Word of God," that ran in the *Pentecostal Herald*, January 1995,

> We need preachers and saints who, with a heart of compassion, will preach against this sin-sick, perverted, immoral generation, and keep their own spirits clean while they fight against the encumbering horror of the invasion of the world upon the church. Paul wrote in I Corinthians 11:1-7 that men are to keep their hair short and that women are to

> have long hair. The passage teaches us that the head of the woman is the man, that she is the glory of the man. When she has long hair as a covering, she appears in the presence of God with glory all over her. I want this world to know that the godly ladies in the United Pentecostal Church are the most beautiful women in the world. They are following sound doctrinal teaching.[4]

Thank you, Brother Urshan, for believing in us, God's women, called, chosen, and faithful to shine forth glory to His name!

4. Nathaniel A. Urshan, "Hearing the Word of God," *Pentecostal Herald*, January 1995, 6-7.

Appendix A

For if the woman be not covered, let her also be shorn: but if it be a shame for a woman to be shorn or shaven, let her be covered (I Corinthians 11:6).

Shorn

Strong's reference number: 2751
Greek: keiro
Derivation: A primary word.
Definition: shear

shear (shîr) v. sheared, sheared or shorn (shôrn, shÅrn), shearing, shears.

—tr.

1. To remove (fleece or hair) by cutting or clipping.
2. To remove the hair or fleece from.
3. To cut with or as if with shears: shearing a hedge.
4. To divest or deprive as if by cutting: The prisoners were shorn of their dignity.

—intr.

1. To use a cutting tool such as shears.
2. To move or proceed by or as if by cutting: shear through the wheat.
3. Physics. To become deformed by forces tending to produce a shearing strain.

—shear n.

1.a. A pair of scissors. Often used in the plural. b. Any of various implements or machines that cut with a scissorlike action. Often used in the plural.

2. The act, process, or result of shearing.

3. Something cut off by shearing.

4. The act, process, or fact of shearing. Used to indicate a sheep's age: a two-shear ram.

5. Also sheers (shîrz). (used with a sing. or pl. verb). An apparatus used to lift heavy weights, consisting of two or more spars joined at the top and spread at the base, the tackle being suspended from the top.

6. Physics. a. An applied force or system of forces that tends to produce a shearing strain. Also called shearing stress, shear stress. b. A shearing strain. [Middle English scheren, from Old English sceran. N., from Middle English shere, from Old English scTar. See sker-1 below.] —shear2er n.

sker-1. Important derivatives are: shear, share1, shears, scabbard, score, shard, short, shirt, skirt, skirmish, screen, carnage, carnal, carnation, carnival, carrion, carnivorous, incarnate, curt, cortex, sharp, scrap1, scrape, scrub1, shrub1, screw.

sker-1. Also ker-. To cut.

I. Basic form *sker-, *ker-.

1.a. SHEAR, from Old English scieran, sceran, to cut; b. SHEER1, from Low German scheren, to move to and fro, and Dutch scheren, to withdraw, depart. Both a and b from Germanic *skeran.

2.a. SHARE2, from Old English scTar, plowshare; b. SHARE1, from Old English scearu, scaru, portion, division (but recorded only in the sense of "fork of the body," "tonsure"). Both a and b from Germanic *skeraz.

3.a. SHEAR, from Old English scTar, scissors, from Germanic *skTr-Å- and *sker-ez-; b. compound *skTr-berg-, "sword protector," scabbard (see bhergh-1). SCABBARD, from Old French escauberc, scabbard, possibly from a Germanic source akin to Old High German scarberc, scabbard. Both a and b from Germanic *skTr-.

4. SCORE, from Old Norse skor, notch, tally, twenty, from Germanic *skur-.

5. SCAR2, SKERRY, from Old Norse sker, low reef (< "something cut off"), from Germanic suffixed form *skar-jam.

6. Suffixed o-grade extended form *skorp-o-. SCARF2, from Old Norse skarfr, diagonally-cut end of a board, from Germanic *skarfaz.

7. Suffixed o-grade extended form *skord-o-. SHARD, from Old

English sceard, a cut, notch, from Germanic *skardaz.

8. Extended form *skerd- in suffixed zero-grade form *skädo-. a. SHORT, from Old English scort, sceort, “cut,” short; b. SHIRT, from Old English scyrte, skirt (< “cut piece”); c. SKIRT, from Old Norse skyrta, shirt. a, b, and c all from Germanic *skurtaz.

9.a. SKIRMISH, from Old French eskermir, to fight with a sword, fence, and Old Italian scaramuccia, skirmish, from a source akin to Old High German skirmen, to protect; b. SCREEN, from Middle Dutch scherm, shield. Both a and b from Germanic extended form *skerm-.

10. Variant form *kar-. CARNAGE, CARNAL, CARNASSIAL, CARNATION, CARNIVAL, CARRION, CARUNCLE, CHARNEL, CRONE; CARNIVOROUS, INCARNATE, from Latin carÅ (stem earn-), flesh.

11. Suffixed o-grade form *kor-yo. CORIACEOUS, CORIUM, CUIRASS, CURRIER; EXCORIATE, from Latin corium, leather (originally “piece of hide”).

12. Suffixed zero-grade form *kä-to-. CURT, CURTAL, KIRTLE, from Latin curtus, short.

13. Suffixed o-grade form *kor-mo-. CORM, from Greek kormos, a trimmed tree trunk.

14. Suffixed o-grade form *kor-I-. COREOPSIS, from Greek koris, bedbug (< “cutter”).

15. Suffixed zero-grade form. SHORE1, from Old English scora, shore, from Germanic *skur-Å.

II. Extended roots *skert-, *kert-.

1. Zero-grade form *kät- or o-grade form *kort-. CORTEX; DECORTICATE, from Latin cortex, bark (< “that which can be cut off”).

2. Suffixed form *kert-snE-. CENACLE, from Latin cTna, meal (< “portion of food”).

III. Extended root *skerp-. SCURF, probably from a Scandinavian source akin to Old English sceorf, scab, scurf, from Germanic *skerf-.

IV. Extended root *skerb(h)-, *skreb(h)-.

1.a. SHARP, from Old English scearp, slope; b. SCARP, from Italian scarpa, embankment, possibly from a Germanic source akin to Gothic skarpÅ, pointed object. Both a and b from Germanic *skarpaz, cutting, sharp.

2.a. SCRAP1, from Old Norse skrap, “pieces,” remains; b. SCRAPE, from Old Norse skrapa, to scratch. Both a and b from Germanic *skrap-.

3.a. SCRABBLE, from Middle Dutch schrabben, to scrape; b. SCRUB1, from Middle Dutch schrobben, to scrape. Both a and b from Germanic *skrab-.

4. SHRUB1, from Old English scrybb, shrub (< “rough plant”), from Germanic *skrub-.

5. SCROBICULATE, from Latin scrobis, trench, ditch.

6. SCREW, SCROFULA, from Latin scrÅfa, a sow (< “rooter, digger”). [Pokorny 4. sker-, Section I. 938.]

Verb: To decrease, as in length or amount, by or as if by severing or excising. cut, reduce, lower, cut back, cut down, slash, trim, chop, crop, curtail, clip, pare, lop.

Clipping (kl≤p2≤ng) n.

Something cut off or out, especially an item clipped from a newspaper or magazine.

clip1 (kl≤p) v. clipped, clipping, clips.

—tr.

1. To cut, cut off, or cut out with or as if with shears: clip coupons; clipped three seconds off the record.

2. To make shorter by cutting; trim: clip a hedge.

3. To cut off the edge of: clip a coin.

4. To cut short; curtail.

5.a. To shorten (a word or words) by leaving out letters or syllables. b. To enunciate with clarity and precision: clip one’s words.

6. Informal. To hit with a sharp blow: clipped me under the eye.

7. Slang. To cheat, swindle, or rob.

—intr.

1. To cut something.

2. Informal. To move rapidly.

—clip1 n.

1. The act of clipping.

2. Something clipped off, especially: a. The wool shorn at one shearing, as of sheep. b. A season's shearing.

3. A short extract from a film or videotape.

4. Informal. A quick, sharp blow: a clip on the ear.

5. Informal. A pace or rate: go at a fast clip.

6. A single occasion; a time: could write nine pages at a clip.

7. clips. A pair of shears or clippers. [Middle English clippen, from Old Norse klippa.]

clip2 (kl≤p) n.

1. Any of various devices for gripping or holding things together; a clasp or fastener.

2. A piece of jewelry that fastens with a clasp or clip; a brooch.

3. A cartridge clip.

4. Football. An act of clipping.

—clip2 tr.v. clipped, clipping, clips.

1. To fasten with or as if with a clip; hold tightly.

2. Football. To block (an opponent who is not carrying the ball) illegally from the rear.

3. Archaic. To embrace or encompass. [Middle English, hook, from clippen, to clasp, embrace, from Old English clyppan.]

Verb: To decrease, as in length or amount, by or as if by severing or excising. cutting, reducing, lowering, cutting back, cutting down, slashing, trimming, chopping, cropping, curtailing, shearing, paring, lopping.

Verb: To join one thing to another. fixing, attaching, connecting, securing, coupling, fastening, affixing, mooring.

Shaven

Strong's reference number: 3587

Greek: xurao
Derivation: Same base as 3586
Definition: to shave

shave (shEv) v. shaved, shaved or shaven (shE2võn), shaving, shaves.

—tr.

1.a. To remove the beard or other body hair from, with a razor or shaver. b. To cut (the beard, for example) at the surface of the skin with a razor or shaver.

2. To crop, trim, or mow closely: shave a meadow.

3.a. To remove thin slices from: shave a board. b. To cut or scrape into thin slices; shred: shave chocolate.

4. To come close to or graze in passing. See Synonyms at brush1.

5.a. To purchase (a note) at a reduction greater than the legal or customary rate. b. To cut (a price) by a slight margin.

—intr.

1. To remove beard or hair with a razor or shaver.

—shave n.

1. The act, process, or result of shaving.

2. A thin slice or scraping; a shaving.

3. Any of various tools used for shaving. [Middle English shaven, to scrape, from Old English sceafan.]

Verb: To cut off a slight amount. trim.

Verb: To make light and momentary contact with, as in passing. glance, brush, kiss, graze.

Verb: To manage with difficulty or so as to barely escape failure. scrape.

Taken from the American Heritage Dictionary and Roget's II Thesaurus CD for Macintosh

Picture Credits

CHAPTER One

ST. CATHERINE CUTTING HER HAIR–Wendy Cooper, *Hair: Sex, Society, Symbolism* (New York: Stein and Day, 1971), 129.

HAIR STYLE OF A ROMAN WOMAN–"Hair," *Illustrated Bible Dictionary*, J. D. Douglas, MA, B.D., S.T.M., PhD (ed.) vol. 2 (1962; Wheaton: Tyndale House, 1980), 603.

FRATERNIZED WOMAN SHAVED–Kappler, Frank K., *Life World War II*, Philip B. Kunjardt Jr. (ed.) (Boston: Little, Brown and Company, 1990), 313.

CHAPTER Two

INDIAN SCALPING ENEMY–Wendy Cooper, *Hair: Sex, Society, Symbolism* (New York: Stein and Day, 1971), 44.

POSTCARD OF THREE WOMEN–The Belle Johnson Collection, Fotofolio. Box 661 Canal Stan., NY, NY 10013.

SEVEN SUTHERLAND SISTERS–John & Alice Durant, *Pic-torial History of the American Circus* (New York: A.S. Barnes and Company, 1955), 121.

CHAPTER Three

CROWN OF LOVE POSTCARD–Statics, Hartman Cards. MARY WASHING THE FEET OF JESUS–Gene Guido 1995.

CHAPTER Four

MAN CARRYING BOY–Robert Payne, *Ancient Greece: The Triumph of a Culture* (New York: W, W. Norton & Company, Inc., 1964).

DECAMERON POSTCARD–Woodmansterne Publications LTD, Watford, ED1 8RD, England.

18TH CENTURY HAIRDO–Wendy Cooper, Hair: Sex Society, Symbolism (New York: Stein and Day, 1971), 148.

CHAPTER Five

VICTORIAN WOMEN–*This Fabulous Century 1870-1900*, Hedley Donovan (ed.) prelude (New York: Time-Life Books, 1970), 190.

CHAPTER Six

IRENE CASTLE–Bill Severn, *The Long and Short of It: 5000 Years of Fun and Fury over Hair*, (New York: David McKay, 1971), 23.

DOES YOUR HAIR REVEAL YOUR CHARACTER?– Popular Mechanics Archives.

MARY PICKFORD–Mary Pickford, "Please May I Bob My Hair?" *Liberty Magazine*, April 1927, *The Liberty Years 1924-1950: An Anthology*, Allen Churchill (ed.) (New Jersey: Prentice-Hall, 1969), 10- 12.

WOMAN GETTING HER HAIR BOBBED–*This Fabulous Century 1920-1930*, Maitland A. Edley (ed.), vol. 3 (New York: Time-Life Books, 1969), 32.

CHAPTER Seven

PUNK ROCKER–Ted Polhemus, Street Style from sidewalk to sidewalk (New York: Thames and Hudson, 1994), 92.

CHAPTER Eight

KING RAMSES II & QUEEN TIY–James Putnam, *Mummy* (1992; New York: Alfred A. Knopf, 1993), 36 & 37.

HAIR & SCALP–Marion Mathews and Renske Mann, *Hair Magic* (New York: Arco Publishing, Inc., 1984), 16.

CROSS SECTION HAIR–Marion Mathews and Renske Mann, Hair Magic (New York: Arco Publishing, Inc., 1984), 17.

LENGTH V EW OF HAIR–Jonathan Zizmor, MD, and John Foreman, Superhair: The Doctor's Book of Beautiful Hair (New York: Berkley, 1978), 16.

FIRST PERM MACHINE–Wendy Cooper, Hair: Sex, Society, Symbolism (New York: Stein and Day, 197A), 18I.

VICTORIAN LADY WITH HAIR DOWN–Larion Mathews and Renske Mann, Hair Magic (New York: Arco Publishing, Inc., 198T).

CHAPTER Nine

HOW DNA FINGERPRINTING WORKS–Ed Timms and Steve McGonigle, "DNA Tests Prove Useful to Defense, Prosecution Alike," *Dallas Morning News*, 11 April 1993, vol. 5, art. 9, 1A.

CHAPTER Ten

AN ALFRESCO TOILET–Woodmansterne Publications LTD, Watford, ED1 8RD, England (1889).

But Why Did I Have to Borrow This Copy?

If that is what you're thinking, you can order additional copies by taking a few minutes to fill out the back of this form. And why not order a book for a friend? I'm sure she would appreciate it. A book is always an appropriate gift. So what are you waiting for? Live seminars are also available by contacting Juli. Make a note on the back of the form. For a prompt response, send it to:

Juli Jasinski
31 North Pepperell Road
Hollis, NH 03049

Titles Available:
My Hair, My Glory, Is there really any significance?
Mi Pelo, Mi Gloria,
Hay Realmente Alguna Importancia?
Daring Dos for Extremely LONG hair
& Basic Hair Care Tips

NEW ITEMS:
Her Ebony Glory: A Tribute to My Sisters of Color

With biblical, historical, and practical information, Juli Jasinski tackles an often overlooked topic. Scripture states that a woman's hair is given to her for her glory. Black ladies often have trouble with their hair not growing. Sister Jasinski offers a thorough history of black women and hair, dispels myths, and offers suggestions for hairdos.

My Hair, My Glory DVD

Juli's book *My Hair, My Glory* comes alive with this seminar. It will encourage, strengthen, and solidify your conviction. The material gained in this seminar will be enough to take back the territory of holiness standards that have been captured by our enemy.

DVD Workbook

Christian Soldiers Workshop TEACHER addition
Christian Soldiers Workshop STUDENT addition
Christian Soldiers Workshop PowerPoint Slides

Check out my website: www.Julisbooks.com